OUR FRIEND FAUSTINA

Life Lessons in Divine Mercy

Edited by
Michele Faehnle & Emily Jaminet

MARIAN PRESS
STOCKBRIDGE MA 01263

Available from:
Marian Helpers Center
Stockbridge, MA 01263

Prayerline: 1-800-804-3823
Orderline: 1-800-462-7426
Websites: TheDivineMercy.org
marian.org

Publisher: Marian Press
ISBN: 978-1-59614-505-4

Publication date: October 5, 2019

Imprimi Potest
Very Rev. Kazimierz Chwalek, MIC
Provincial Superior
The Blessed Virgin Mary, Mother of Mercy Province
January 16, 2019

Nihil Obstat
Dr. Robert A. Stackpole, STD
Censor Deputatus
January 16, 2019

Early Praise for
Our Friend Faustina

Every once in a while, a book comes along to fill a deep hole in your heart and lead you into the light. *Our Friend Faustina* offers every reader this gift. A beautiful compendium of work by talented authors, this resource meets every reader exactly where they are along their spiritual journey and offers them the solace, mercy, support, and hope of a trusted new friend: Saint Faustina. Whether you already have a devotion to the Divine Mercy or are wanting accompaniment for your journey into St. Faustina's profound spirituality, Michele Faehnle, Emily Jaminet, and their co-authors provide a terrific spiritual tool. Fall in love with a new friend, St. Faustina, as she walks alongside you on your journey to Jesus Christ.

> — **Lisa M. Hendey,** founder of CatholicMom.com
> and author of *I Am God's Storyteller.*

Whether you are new to the life and literature of St. Faustina Kowalska or you consider her one of your dearest friends and intercessors, *Our Friend Faustina: Life Lessons in Divine Mercy* will inspire your faith, grow your trust, and strengthen your devotion to Jesus' Divine Mercy.

> — **Katie Warner,** author of *Head & Heart: Becoming*
> *Spiritual Leaders for Your Family* and the
> FirstFaithTreasury.com series

Our Friend Faustina: Life Lessons in Divine Mercy is an inspiring collection of women's voices, all speaking from different perspectives about the same truth: St. Faustina is a heavenly friend who is alive and working among us, acting in our lives and spreading her message of Jesus' mercy and love. Reading through, one essay at a time, is an educational, inspirational retreat of Divine Mercy.

> — **Danielle Bean,** Brand Manager, Catholicmom.com

With the Year of Mercy a distant memory, Divine Mercy had, for me, become "ho-hum" and Faustina. . . who?. . . I had lost that zeal, that fervent devotion. I was needing to be schooled. That's when this little book fell into my hands. These "Life Lessons" were just what my lukewarm heart needed. I was moved by the encouraging stories of how others came to be devoted, how they were sought and befriended by St. Faustina. The beautiful prayers closing each chapter further rekindled my joy and love to this saint and devotion to Divine Mercy. If your Divine Mercy devotion has become tired and St. Faustina needs to be "friended" again, then let *Our Friend Faustina: Life Lessons in Divine Mercy* teach you to love them anew.

— **Tami Kiser,** author of *Smart Martha's Catholic Guide for Busy Moms* teacher, speaker, producer, and founder of Heart Ridge Catholic Family Ministries

*Dedicated to
our friend and companion,
St. Faustina.*

CONTENTS

FOREWORD

Our Friend Faustina is a wonderful introduction to St. Faustina who — as these 11 writers explain — introduced herself to them.

Yes, that's possible! The same thing happened to me over the past five years as I read, researched, and wrote about the Diary of this amazing nun and visionary.

I "discovered" St. Faustina and her *Diary* in the early '80s — before she was a household name in the United States — and her writing fascinated me. And I think she knew what was to come when I found myself at her canonization on April 30, 2000!

Promoting prayers for the Holy Souls in Purgatory has long been a personal mission dear to my heart, but it was Fr. Dan Cambra of the Marian Fathers of the Immaculate Conception who, some six years ago, suggested writing about that in relation to St. Faustina's *Diary*. Books on conversion, Adoration, and day-by-day spirituality followed. All based on the wonderful message of Divine Mercy.

On a more personal level, reading St. Faustina's words has been like meeting a wonderful new friend who's so approachable, warm, and caring. At the same time, her *Diary* reveals that she, too, had her share of suffering. Hers was not a charmed life ... but a blessed one.

Now I'm so pleased and honored to be writing the foreword for *Our Friend Faustina*.

In it you'll see how, more than just coming to know her, the authors came to discover how what she wrote in her *Diary* could also describe a part of, or situation in, their own lives. How it could deeply influence the ways they chose to live that part, that situation, with a sense of spirituality, a sense of service, and a sense of striving to do God's will.

Each in her own way.

These women, these writers, are to be commended for sharing their fascinating stories with us and for giving readers a wonderful mix of St. Faustina's revelations, prayers, and — truly — invaluable advice and example for living in today's world as a strong and committed Catholic.

I have no doubt you'll enjoy and benefit from what you find here. I did.

Susan Tassone
Author of:
Day by Day with St. Faustina: 365 Reflections
St. Faustina Prayer Book for Adoration
St. Faustina Prayer Book for the Conversion of Sinners
St. Faustina Prayer Book for the Holy Souls in Purgatory

Stockbridge, Mass — Dr. Joseph
Shrine of Divine Mercy

INTRODUCTION

Saint Maria Faustina Kowalska (1905-1938) is one of the most popular saints of modern times. During her canonization Mass in April of 2000, Pope John Paul II described her as a "gift of God to our time"[1] and as one of the Church's great mystics. Her work on earth was to spread God's merciful love across the world, yet her influence did not end with her death. Before she passed into eternal life, St. Faustina wrote in her *Diary*, "I feel certain that my mission will not come to an end upon my death, but will begin. O doubting souls, I will draw aside for you the veils of heaven to convince you of God's goodness, so that you will no longer continue to wound with your distrust the sweetest Heart of Jesus" (*Diary of Saint Maria Faustina Kowalska*, 281).

Since her death in 1938, thousands of miracles have been attributed to her intercession and millions of people have been impacted by her writings. I, too, was greatly affected by her life and message. At first glance, this humble Polish saint, born into a poor family in the early 1900s, didn't seem to have much in common with my life as a modern woman living in America, yet as I began to read the writings of this great saint, my life started to change. Saint Faustina's life and spirituality have had a profound effect on my own journey, and I have felt her gentle hands encouraging me to spread the devotion to Divine Mercy as she continues her mission in eternity. I am not the only one whom this great saint has influenced. Saint Faustina has impacted millions with her writings.

Our Friend Faustina is another example of her powerful intercession before the throne of God, and her desire to see the message of Divine Mercy spread across the world. When Emily and I were approached by Chris Sparks of Marian Press in the summer of 2017 to assemble a compilation book of essays from women who were influenced by St. Faustina's spirituality, I thought, "Well, it sounds like a nice idea, but there is no way I can fit this into my schedule right now." I had just accepted a full-time job after being a stay-at-home mom for five years, and knew my writing time would be limited. I told St. Faustina that this was not the time; someone else could do the job. Yet, both Emily and I felt called in prayer to do this work, despite all the material obstacles. After discussing the idea with Marian Press, we agreed to move forward with the project.

In order for it to come to fruition, though, I needed certain elements to come together, so I prayed to St. Faustina and gave her a few conditions that she would have to intercede for and make happen. First, the women I felt called in prayer to approach about contributing to the project had to give a resounding "yes." Second, the book proposal had to be completed by the time I returned to work after the two-and-a-half-week Christmas break.

After much prayer, I sent emails to my friends in the writing world who I knew had a connection to St. Faustina, asking for their participation. In less than 24 hours, every woman but one replied with a "YES." These women were not only agreeable, but even ecstatic to participate in the project and share their stories. I knew God's hand was at work.

With my contributors set, I began the task of finishing the book proposal. I had 16 days off before I would have to return to full-time work. Although that amount of time originally seemed adequate, the busyness of the Christmas season gave me less working time than I had anticipated. I was about a thousand words short on my sample chapter and had quite a bit of editing to do by the end of the 16th day of break. As I packed my lunch and put my scrubs out in preparation for work the next morning, I was too exhausted to stay up late and finish the proposal. I told St. Faustina, "Well, you are just going to have to give me some time tomorrow," and gave myself a one-day extension. I was hoping for a slow day at the office or a few hours after school to wrap things up. At 6:15 the next morning, I awoke to my alarm clock and picked up my cell phone. I noticed that I had several text messages waiting to be read. I could hardly believe the **URGENT** message that the little gray box proclaimed: "School cancelled due to icy conditions." A bonus day was given to me from my friend in Heaven! So there I sat, on a cold snowy day, writing about my friend Faustina instead of going back to work!

As an added bonus, I also felt compelled to ask my friend Derya Little, author of *From Islam to Christ*, to contribute her story to the compilation. She not only agreed, but helped me along the way with editing and ideas to complete the project. The final "little miracle" was when I reached out to a distant relative, Kelly (Faehnle) Sheredy on Facebook. After a few pleasant conversations, we became quick friends and, as an English major with editing experience, she, too, joined the team to make this work possible.

In the pages ahead of you, you will meet 11 women and hear their stories of how St. Faustina has inspired them to grow closer to Jesus and trust in Him, and to live out God's will in their lives. These are stories of faith, hope, trust, and mercy, stories of ordinary women who, like St. Faustina (and with some heavenly aid), gave a little "yes" that changed their lives forever. It is our hope that these words lead you to love Jesus as St. Faustina does. May her prayer be answered: "O my Jesus ... I would like the whole world to be transformed into love for You, my Betrothed" (*Diary*, 1771).

CHAPTER 1

Tapped on the Shoulder by St. Faustina

Michele Faehnle

Sometimes we speak to the saints, begging their intercession before the throne of God; other times, however, the saints speak to us, asking us to continue the good works they began on earth. Our heavenly friends who have gone before us are not far removed from us; rather, they are still part of our lives. As *Lumen Gentium (Dogmatic Constitution on the Church)* says, their friendship is not "weakened or interrupted" by their death, but instead, strengthened by the bonds of our faith and "communication of spiritual goods."[2]

I've been blessed to have friendships with many of the saints in Heaven, but St. Faustina has become an extra special confidante and guide to me. She is one of those saints that came into my life and "tapped me on the shoulder," if you will, to push me to greater holiness and to be a part of her great mission to spread the message of God's great mercy across the world. I was introduced to her as a young girl in the 1990s, when my parents first learned of the devotion to Divine Mercy. We attended Divine Mercy Sunday celebrations even when they were only offered at a handful of parishes in the United States and Faustina was still known as "Blessed" by the Catholic Church. (Part of the process the Catholic Church uses to recognize people as saints, this is the step before canonization). We prayed the Chaplet of Divine Mercy each day and had the large image of Jesus with red and pale rays on our mantle over the fireplace. Honestly, I was drawn to the devotion mainly because the Chaplet was shorter than the Rosary; plus, I knew of the promises given to St. Faustina that those who participated in Divine Mercy Sunday celebrations by going to Confession and receiving Holy Communion would receive total remission of all sin and punishment (see *Diary*, 1109). In my immature spirituality as a young teenager, I thought this was my "get out of jail free" card to live my life as I pleased and yet still be able to squeak into Heaven. As I grew in my faith I came to understand what the devotion to Divine Mercy truly was — a great invitation to God's mercy and a call to deep conversion. Much later in life, I dove into the *Diary of Saint Maria Faustina Kowalska*, and as I pored through many biographical works on her life, this acquaintanceship grew into a true spiritual friendship.

Who is St. Faustina?

Sister Maria Faustina was born Helen Kowalska in 1905 to a poor family in Głogowiec, Poland, the third of 10 children. She was a very pious and prayerful young girl and had a special place in her heart for the sufferings of others.

Young Helen knew she was called to religious life as early as age 7. She grew in holiness despite the fact she could not always attend Sunday Mass because the family only owned one Sunday dress, which was shared by the girls. She learned to read and write from her father and later went to school. Although she was a good student, she was forced to leave school after only two years to make room for younger students. At age 14 she moved in with another family to become a domestic servant. It was there she received a vision of a bright light and felt called to join the convent.

At first, her parents did not want her to join the convent, so she went back to work as a housekeeper. But Jesus was persistent in His call. When she was 18, Helen experienced a vision of Jesus, who asked of her, **"How long shall I put up with you and how long will you keep putting Me off?"** (*Diary*, 9).

After being refused by several orders, Helen finally was accepted into the Congregation of the Sisters of Our Lady of Mercy in Warsaw in 1925. Soon after, she took her religious name: Sr. Maria Faustina of the Most Blessed Sacrament.

Initially, she thought she might be called to leave this order for a stricter order, but Jesus made it clear to her that she was where he wanted her to be. Faustina made her vows with the Sisters of Our Lady of Mercy and served as a cook, gardener, and doorkeeper. She stayed in several different convents, but mainly at the convents in Kraków, Płock, and Vilnius. During much of her life in the convent she was in ill health, as she suffered from tuberculosis, a terrible disease of the lungs. She never complained about her suffering, though, instead offering it to Jesus for the poor souls in Purgatory. In her simple life in the convent; she was obedient and cheerful and did her daily tasks with great love. She had a very meek and humble manner, and the sisters described her as always having "childlike joy on her face."[3] Faustina suffered greatly, though. Not only did she have the physical pain associated with tuberculosis, but during her novitiate she also underwent a great "dark night of the soul," a phrase coined by St. John of the Cross that describes a deep spiritual pain experienced by some as they grow in spiritual maturity and union with God. This trial lasted almost until the end of her novitiate.

In 1931, she was staying at the convent in Płock when she received the vision of the Risen Christ in a white robe, with one hand raised in blessing and the other hand touching His heart. Two rays of light streamed from His chest: one red and one pale, like the color of a fountain of water. Jesus instructed her to have Him painted as she saw Him and to see that the portrait was spread around the world (*Diary*, 47–48). When she first reported this request to her confessor, he told Faustina that Jesus just wanted her to paint His image in her soul; however, in another vision, Jesus confirmed that He wanted a material image created.

Faustina asked a sister in the convent if she would be able to paint the image for her. This sister declined, but word spread around the convent that Faustina was receiving visions. While a few of the sisters believed in her extraordinary experiences, Faustina wrote in her *Diary* that many "began to speak openly about me and to regard me as a hysteric and a fantasist, and the rumors began to grow louder" (*Diary*, 125). Some of the sisters were very cruel and humiliated her publicly, but Faustina kept her peace and never uttered anything in her defense.

After moving to the convent at Vilnius, she was soon blessed with a spiritual advisor, Fr. Michael Sopocko, who would help her fulfill her mission. After a doctor evaluated Faustina's physical and mental health and vouched for her sanity, Fr. Sopocko helped find an artist, Eugeniusz Kazimirowski, to paint the picture under Faustina's direction. She visited the artist each weekend to instruct him and was often dissatisfied. The painting was changed several times by Kazimirowski. In 1934, the painting was almost finished, but Sr. Faustina was still not pleased. She went to the chapel and cried. She asked Jesus, "Who will paint You as beautiful as You are?" In response she heard, "**Not in the beauty of the color, nor of the brush lies the greatness of this image, but in My grace**" (*Diary*, 313). After 12 tries, Sr. Faustina accepted the painting, saying, "It is not what it should be, but that's how it must remain."[4] The Divine Mercy Image was first displayed publicly on the Friday after Easter in 1935 at the Shrine of Our Lady of Ostra Brama in Vilnius, where Fr. Sopocko gave a sermon about Divine Mercy. While he was preaching, Sr. Faustina saw the image come alive, and the "rays pierced the hearts of the people gathered there" (*Diary*, 417).

Jesus continued to appear to Faustina and reveal His mission for her. In the *Diary*, she recorded the words Jesus spoke to her, "**I am sending you with My mercy to the people of the whole world**" (*Diary*, 1588). What we know of her experiences is recorded in her *Diary*, which she continued to write until she died in 1938 from tuberculosis. She was only 33.[5]

My Friend Faustina

As a nurse who only took three English courses in college, I never dreamed I would someday write a book. I am still in awe that this is my third book, and the second one about one of the most popular and greatest mystics of the Catholic Church, St. Faustina. I also never imagined that I would travel the United States sharing the message of Divine Mercy with anyone who would listen, yet in the two years following the printing of *Divine Mercy for Moms*,[6] I have spoken on the Eternal Word Television Network (EWTN), countless radio programs, retreats, and conferences about my friend Faustina and her mission of mercy.

In hindsight, I realize that I did seek the help of this saint long ago. Over 20 years ago, I found myself kneeling beside her tomb in Krakow, Poland. I was 19 years old and studying abroad at the time. I took this weekend trip mainly because Poland offered inexpensive food, a fun nightlife, and cheap souvenirs. Coming from a family of Polish descent, I felt as though this side trip to Poland was also important to understand my heritage. I visited St. Faustina's convent because "all the other students were doing it." As it was still early in my personal conversion process, this little religious pilgrimage was squeezed in between shopping for amber, indulging in Polish delicatessens, and partying in the discotheques. Yet when I read my journal from that weekend in 1996, it should not have been surprising to see that out of all the fun I had that weekend, "the best part of the trip was going to Sr. Faustina's convent and praying the Chaplet of Divine Mercy at 3 p.m. in front of the tomb of Sr. Faustina." She was only recognized as Blessed Faustina at that time and not as well-known as she is today, but the influence of this humble sister had an undeniable impact on me that would resonate into my adult life.

Fast-forward 17 years from that fateful weekend trip, and again I found myself meeting with this saint, as I decided to spend the summer reading the *Diary*. My friend Faustina spoke to me in ways that would change my spirituality forever.

The following are three particularly poignant lessons my friend, Faustina, taught me.

Complete Surrender to the Will of God.

> Now I understand well that what unites our soul most closely to God is self-denial; that is, joining our will to the will of God (*Diary*, 462).

Anyone who knows me can tell you that I have a type A personality. I like my life to be organized, thought-out, and running according to how I think it should go. I always have a plan A, plan B, and plan C. Being open to what God has in store for me, instead of only what I have planned, has been quite a challenge for my life. Every day, He asks me to do simple things, yet my desire to do things my own way sometimes wins over. Molding my will to His is not an easy thing to do! Saint Faustina's writings have been instrumental in helping me "let go and let God" so that He can work in my life.

One of my favorite passages in the *Diary* is number 374. It's a unique page in this book because a large X covers the entire page. In the middle of the X, St. Faustina writes, "From today on, my own will does not exist." On the next page, the only thing written on a blank page is "From today on, I do the Will of God everywhere, always, and in everything" (*Diary*, 374). Because of this entry, I have now made it a priority each morning when I grab my coffee to say this simple prayer: "Dear Lord, conform my will to Yours, and do not let my will get in the way of Yours." This powerful supplication each morning has brought about drastic change in my life.

One of those changes is that I began writing Catholic books, even though my profession was nursing. I was very proud of my job as a nurse, and it was an important part of my identity. I can see now how God had to pry my nursing career out of my hands in order to help me grow spiritually. As my family grew, I gradually worked less and less, until I decided to put nursing on pause. I was happy with the change. The extra time I had could be spent co-chairing our diocesan Catholic

Women's Conference, volunteering, and spending time with my family. Little did I know, God had a greater plan.

A few years later, I was invited to speak at the National Shrine of Divine Mercy in Stockbridge, Massachusetts, and share my testimony of mercy and trust in God. I remember staring across the sea of people gathered to celebrate Divine Mercy Sunday and asking, "Why me, Lord? Why ask a simple mom to stand before all these people and share about Your mercy?" As I finished my talk and stepped down from the podium, one of the other guests asked, "Are you a professional speaker? You did such a wonderful job and I could tell you were not nervous at all!" I chuckled at her comment and shook my head as I explained that I was really a nurse and this was the first time I had spoken in front of such a large crowd. I would later come to understand that this was a moment of great grace for myself and my family. Saint Faustina was at work again.

Shortly after I returned from Stockbridge, I was contacted by an editor at Ave Maria Press and asked to write a book about Divine Mercy and motherhood. Pregnant at the time with my fourth child, I laughed at the idea. As an experienced mother, I was aware that a new baby meant that I would be lucky to get a shower every day; there was no way that I would have time to write a book! Yet St. Faustina continued to tap away. This time, she also tapped my friend, Emily Jaminet, on the shoulder to help me with the project. Emily agreed to help me co-author the manuscript, and *Divine Mercy for Moms* was born. As we launched our book, we also began to speak around the country on the topic, "Our Friend Faustina, Lessons of Mercy for Life." We could hardly believe that God was using us, two little moms, to share the message of Divine Mercy! Yet, as all who follow Him know, those who seek God's will are always fulfilled in ways they would never have imagined. I came to understand what St. Faustina shares in her *Diary*: "True love of God consists in carrying out God's will. To show God our love in what we do, all our actions, even the least, must spring from our love of God" (*Diary*, 279).

In keeping with God's wonderful sense of humor, last year I was given the opportunity to go back to work as a school nurse at a Catholic school just five minutes away from my home! I can now see how God wants me to do both careers, but not out of love for myself or how I may appear to others, but instead, out of love for Him.

Difficult Tasks Done with Love are a Gift to God

Saint Faustina belonged to the Congregation of the Sisters of Our Lady of Mercy. One of the main charisms of the order was taking care of wayward girls (prostitutes) who needed moral conversion. They gave them both spiritual and corporal help to aid them in changing their lives. It was an active community, and the sisters were divided into two "choirs." The sisters who were educated were in the first choir, which took care of teaching the girls whom they served. Saint Faustina was with the non-educated sisters in the second choir, which supported all the sisters and the girls by cooking, cleaning, and gardening. Having poor health, these tasks could be difficult for St. Faustina, as one of my favorite stories from the *Diary* recounts:

> One time during the novitiate ... I was very upset because I could not manage the pots, which were very large. The most difficult task for me was draining the potatoes, and sometimes I spilt half of them with the water. ... I complained to God about my weakness. Then I heard the following words in my soul, **"From today on you will do this easily; I shall strengthen you."**
>
> That evening, when the time came to drain off the water from the potatoes, I hurried to be the first to do it, trusting in the Lord's words. I took up the pot with ease and poured off the water perfectly. But when I took off the cover to let the potatoes steam off, I saw there in the pot, in the place of

the potatoes, whole bunches of red roses, beautiful beyond description. ... I heard a voice within me saying, **"I change such hard work of yours into bouquets of most beautiful flowers, and their perfume rises up to My throne"** (*Diary*, 65).

I love how this story reminds me to do my daily tasks with great love. The small things like cooking, cleaning, and other thankless chores that are often unnoticed by the world, are the most beautiful bouquets to our Lord. My life is not a glamorous one. I spend more hours working at the kitchen sink and in the laundry room than doing anything of great importance. It is so easy for me to become resentful while doing this work instead of offering it to the Lord. A friend gave me a beautiful idea, though: Instead of allowing anger and resentment to build while hard at work at the sink, she suggested that I put a prayer card in my window that I could read while doing the dishes. Now my "sink prayer" is a holy card with the "Prayer of Divine Transformation from Within" from the *Diary* of St. Faustina. It's a lengthy, but powerful, prayer that you'll find at the end of this chapter, but this line sums up its message: "I want to be completely transformed into Your mercy and to be Your living reflection, O Lord" (*Diary*, 163). As I scrub my dishes clean, this beautiful prayer by St. Faustina has helped me transform my dirty soul into a vessel of mercy!

Closeness to Mary Will Draw You to Jesus

Saint Faustina had a deep devotion to the Blessed Mother and knew that living by her example she could more perfectly love Jesus and do His will. She wrote in her *Diary*, "I have been living under the virginal cloak of the Mother of God. She has been guarding me and instructing me. I am quite at peace, close to Her Immaculate Heart. Because I am so weak and inexperienced, I nestle like a little child close to Her heart"

(*Diary*, 1097). Saint Faustina also wrote in her *Diary* about Mary's understanding of our suffering. The Blessed Mother told her, "*I know how much you suffer, but do not be afraid. I share with you your suffering, and I shall always do so*" (*Diary*, 25).

Although I had consecrated myself to Mary as a young girl, it wasn't until I was an adult and using Fr. Michael Gaitley's *33 Days to Morning Glory*[7] that I began to understand Mary's role in my life, especially in my suffering.

The turning point in my understanding of suffering came, tragically, in the form of a very difficult miscarriage. The physical symptoms had been so traumatic that I didn't have time to process the emotional side of the loss. I was planning on traveling to visit Fr. Michael Gaitley, MIC, a friend who was speaking just a few hours away, but I was now unable to drive that long of a distance.

When I shared the sorrowful news, he wrote back, "Have you named the baby?"

"I hadn't even had time to think about it," I texted him back.

"I'll be praying for you. Take some time, rest and reflect if you can," was his reply.

I knew exactly what I needed to do. I had been prompted several times recently to reconsecrate myself to Mary using *33 Days to Morning Glory*, and I knew that the Lord was asking me to do so right then.

As I prayed and pondered through the reflections each day, I was overcome with the peace and joy that could only be brought to me by Mary, placing me in the arms of Jesus. Mary, who knew suffering and the loss of a child, came to my aid. I named the baby and asked Mary to give the baby to my Nana (my great grandmother, who had passed away when I was in college) to watch over until I could see him in Heaven someday.

On the Feast of the Assumption, I had just texted Fr. Gaitley to thank him for his advice, telling him how *33 Days to Morning Glory* had brought healing to my soul, when the doorbell rang. An unexpected gift from my Aunt Penny had arrived. I opened the package and the letter read:

> Dear Michele,
> While going through my books, I found this one —
> it was Nana's prayer book. As soon as I saw it, the
> thought came to me that I should give it to you.
> After having that thought, I opened the book and
> this picture fell out (Author's Note: It was a picture
> of me from the sixth grade). I knew it was meant
> for you!

With tears of sorrow, joy, and peace, I began to weep. I thanked Mary for this special gift on her feast day, a kiss from Heaven, and the special touch of my great-grandmother. I couldn't have asked for a more meaningful present.

As I unwrapped the prayer book, I stared with disbelief at its title. In college, I belonged to a household group (a spirit-led community of women at my college, sort of like a Catholic sorority) named after the Blessed Mother: Mother of Love. Scripted in gold on the front cover were the words, *Mother Love.*

Life on earth will always have suffering. We cannot escape it, no matter how hard we try; but if we allow Mary into our hearts, she will use this suffering to make us more like Christ, and I can attest, she will make it sweet. Saint Faustina wrote this beautiful prayer to Our Lady in her *Diary* that I pray as a reminder of my consecration:

> O Mary, my Mother and my Lady, I offer You my
> soul, my body, my life and my death, and all that
> will follow it. I place everything in Your hands. O
> my Mother, cover my soul with your virginal man-
> tle and grant me the grace of purity of heart, soul,
> and body. Defend me with Your power against all
> enemies, and especially against those who hide their
> malice behind the mask of virtue. O lovely lily! You
> are for me a mirror, O my Mother! (*Diary*, 79)

I am still a young pupil in St. Faustina's school of spirituality. Each day, her example leads me closer to Jesus and encourages me to dive deeper into the ocean of mercy. As I learn more about her childlike trust in God and her desire to grow in holiness by being merciful to her neighbor, I have grown in my desire to be an active witness of mercy.

Saint Faustina, pray for us!

Portions of this chapter were originally published in a book by Michele Faehnle and Emily Jaminet, *Divine Mercy for Moms: Sharing the Lessons of St. Faustina* (Notre Dame, IN: Ave Maria Press, 2015). Used with permission.

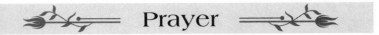

Prayer

A prayer for divine transformation from within.

O Most Holy Trinity! As many times as I breathe, as many time as my heart beats, as many times as my blood pulsates through my body, so many thousand times do I want to glorify Your mercy.

I want to be completely transformed into Your mercy and to be Your living reflection, O Lord. May the greatest of all divine attributes, that of Your unfathomable mercy, pass through my heart and soul to my neighbor.

Help me, O Lord, that my eyes may be merciful, so that I may never suspect or judge from appearances, but look for what is beautiful in my neighbors' souls and come to their rescue.

Help me, that my ears may be merciful, so that I may give heed to my neighbors' needs and not be indifferent to their pains and moanings.

Help me, O Lord, that my tongue may be merciful, so that I should never speak negatively of my neighbor, but have a word of comfort and forgiveness for all.

Help me, O Lord, that my hands may be merciful and filled with good deeds, so that I may do only good to my neighbors and take upon myself the more difficult and toilsome tasks.

Help me, that my feet may be merciful, so that I may hurry to assist my neighbor, overcoming my own fatigue and weariness. My true rest is in the service of my neighbor.

Help me, O Lord, that my heart may be merciful so that I myself may feel all the sufferings of my neighbor. I will refuse my heart to no one. I will be sincere even with those who, I know, will abuse my kindness. And I will lock myself up in the most merciful Heart of Jesus. I will bear my own suffering in silence. May Your mercy, O Lord, rest upon me. Amen. (*Diary*, 163)

CHAPTER 2

Life Lessons Learned from Faustina

Emily Jaminet

My journey with St. Faustina began with a devotion that was practiced in my own family three decades ago. I still remember holding the Rosary beads in my hand to learn the Chaplet of Divine Mercy in high school. Over the years, this devotion has blossomed into a spirituality that not only has brought me closer to Jesus and His Divine Mercy, but also has served as a compass to help me navigate my earthly journey. Thanks to this devotion, I pray more intensely, seek out God's mercy more often, and believe that our God is a God worth trusting.

Saint Faustina brought the Chaplet of Divine Mercy to the world as a way to touch the hardest of hearts and help usher in a new era of grace for a people who lack both faith and trust in God. I am forever grateful for this lifeline of spirituality discovered in my youth and have continued to practice this devotion throughout my adult life. I invoked St. Faustina's intercession as a young teenager, a new bride, a mother with a house full of young children, and now parenting toddlers to teens. Through it all, I have seen distinct instances in my life of direct divine intervention that have not only taught me a lesson, but also showed me the miracles that can take place when you open yourself up to God's mercy.

I feel privileged to have known this saint while she was just a "blessed." Thanks to the invitation of a friend while in a college study abroad program, I was fortunate enough to travel to Poland to visit the convent where St. Faustina spent her days serving others and praying. I am confident that the prayers I offered at her convent that day were heard and answered. My experience there inspired me to join in the mission to promote this devotion and live out St. Faustina's spirituality. Since that time, I have learned more about St. Faustina's childlike trust in God and her desire to grow in holiness by being merciful to her neighbor as I pondered the words in her *Diary*. As she poured out her heart and soul in the pages of this book, Jesus came alive as if He were speaking directly to me.

This humble saint from Poland allowed herself to be emptied out for God, and in return He filled her with a personal and intimate relationship with Him through an active daily prayer life and a life of service and care for others. Saint Faustina has taught me over the years that I need to seek out God's graces for living a life rooted in trust of His Divine Mercy. In the *Diary*, Jesus instructs, **"Your duty is to trust entirely in My Mercy, My duty is to give you all that you need. I make Myself dependent on your trust: if your trust is great, then My generosity will be without limit"** (*Diary*, 548). Furthermore, I have learned to be open to the many opportunities throughout my day to perform the works of mercy, no matter how big or small they might seem at the time, to help bring mercy and love to others both inside and outside my home.

Becoming a Woman of Prayer

Saint Faustina lived a life where prayer was her fuel for her daily duties. She spent several hours each day in prayer, attending daily Mass, saying the Rosary, praying the Divine Office, and going to Adoration on top of carrying out her duties at the convent. It was to these things that she felt most attracted. Saint Faustina longed for a more contemplative prayer life, and yet Jesus told her that He had distinct graces to offer through her calling with the Sisters of Mercy and her daily work there. Saint Faustina said that, after receiving Communion, she repeatedly felt Jesus' distinct presence in her soul for quite some time. This presence was a great consolation to her as she struggled through her daily routine. Jesus accompanied her everywhere. She went to work and had recreation time with Him, rejoiced with Him and suffered with Him. She worked in the kitchen, answered the door, labored in the garden and served the community of girls under their care. "His company meant that she did not feel alone, abandoned."[8] This deep prayer life was where she would draw the strength to live a life of service to others.

Saint Faustina has taught me through her example that prayer provides the strength we need to serve and care for those around us. Prayer needs to be our daily fuel as it was for St. Faustina. Despite how difficult it can be to find the time to pray, it is essential to carve out time for daily prayer that is quiet and reflective so that you can go forth to live a life on the go. I have discovered over the years that "you cannot give what you do not have." Without prayer, it is all too easy to become mired in our daily routine and lose our eternal perspective. At the same time, as a laywoman, my prayer life must reflect my vocation and stage in life, and I must resist the temptation to resent those duties that are an integral part of it. If this great saint could learn from Christ Himself to combine her work with continual prayer, we can be inspired to do the same with our tasks and duties. While praying in this way may not be a direct replacement for quiet, contemplative prayer, it still has value.

As a working mother of seven children, there are times I would prefer to be immersed in quiet, reflective prayer rather than carrying out my daily duties of working, doing laundry, cleaning, cooking, and providing for others. I know how hard it can be to take time out to reflect and pray. I quickly came to realize, however, that consistent prayer is important and is not something to be put off until life slows down. I was especially guilty of neglecting regular prayer while my first three children were young, often waiting for a quiet time to be with the Lord instead of allowing my prayer to take place in union with my vocation and my daily duties. I wasted a lot of time feeling frustrated with my vocation since I thought it was preventing me from growing in holiness rather than providing an opportunity to seek out new graces to love and serve. Now, I try to unite my vocation as a wife and mother with prayer that fuels my daily activities and provides me with new graces. Each day I endeavor to remember that my goal is the same as St. Faustina's — to know, love and serve Christ in the hope of being with Him in Heaven for all of eternity.

Saint Faustina mentioned many times in her *Diary* that Christ wants to offer us a personal relationship with Him. **"[W]ith childlike simplicity talk to Me about everything, for My ears and heart are inclined towards you, and your words are dear to Me"** (*Diary*, 921). We can begin by knowing that we are God's children, and that He wants us to come to Him. We must go to Him and lay our burdens down, no matter what is on our minds or where we are in the day. We can talk to Jesus as we are driving in the car, running on the treadmill, doing the laundry, or stirring dinner in the Crock-Pot. Giving Christ prayer time is essential to growing in a deep and real relationship with Him. Jesus longs for our attention and wants us to develop an authentic relationship with Him; it is essential to speak to Christ in prayer about our daily happenings, pouring our hearts out to Him, and taking time to hear Him speak in our innermost beings. Saint Faustina had an unbelievable relationship with Christ in which He presented himself as Lord, Savior, and friend. We, too, can have that type of relationship if we take time out to cultivate a deep prayer life.

Living a Life of Mercy

Another significant lesson I learned from St. Faustina is her example of living a life of mercy. She wrote these words from Jesus in her *Diary*: **"I am giving you three ways of exercising mercy toward your neighbor: the first — by deed, the second — by word, the third — by prayer. In these**

three degrees is contained the fullness of mercy, and it is an unquestionable proof of love for Me. By this means a soul glorifies and pays reverence to My mercy" (*Diary*, 742).

God calls us to serve our families inside our homes and others outside our homes, but how can we create time to do works of mercy when we already have so much on our shoulders? Dealing with our responsibilities provides a beautiful opportunity to learn how to access new graces that will help us to manage our lives; we must learn to turn the whole day over to Christ and be open to His holy will. One of the most profound examples of learning to live a life of mercy began when my friend Megan called me one day.

"I think there is someone you should meet," she said. "My friend Mike is sick and becoming increasingly more paralyzed each day. He needs to have a friend like you, since you have young children to brighten his day."

Mike, once a successful lawyer and Harvard football player, was in his early 30s at the time and had been diagnosed with Amyotrophic Lateral Sclerosis (ALS), also known as Lou Gehrig's disease. This two-time football letter winner and All-Ivy League Honorable Mention selection in the late 1980s was now being moved out of his apartment to live the rest of his life in a long-term care facility.

I decided to meet Mike at the request of my friend, despite the fact that my own life as a happily married woman and mother of six young children was full enough. When I took a moment to consider his life, I knew that I couldn't just turn my back and walk away. Once highly successful from the world's standpoint, now he could no longer do even simple things like turn the pages on a newspaper, brush his teeth, or even walk to the bathroom. Over 6 feet 4 inches tall, Mike was not a small person, and yet he had been crammed into an average hospital bed for years, suffering, waiting, and working to find new ways to manage his disease.

My family began to visit Mike regularly, and putting all of us together was a recipe for success, just as my friend had anticipated. At this time in my life, I had a houseful of young children eager for others' attention, and Mike was a great person to pay them a lot of it, receiving their undying affection in return. My young boys played football and loved to discuss sports with him, while my very little ones sang and danced to show off their talents.

Over the course of several years, we visited Mike here and there and for special occasions. The one event every year for which we would go out of our way to see Mike was his birthday. Megan, my friend who had introduced us, would bring us all together to help Mike blow out his candles — literally — and sing another round or two of "Happy Birthday." Even with all these sweet memories, we soon found that God was calling our friendship to something even deeper.

Spiritual Friendship

I knew that I was meant to be in Mike's life when I showed up one day to visit him while he needed extra care at a local Catholic hospital. For some reason, perhaps to get something for Mike, I opened his top dresser drawer and found a consecrated Host — the Holy Eucharist! Apparently, a visiting Extraordinary Minister had stopped by to offer Mike Holy Communion, but seeing him asleep, decided not to wake him and placed the Body of Christ in his drawer, something he could not even reach! We both knew that this was not acceptable, no matter how well-meaning the man might have been. At the time I didn't know what exactly to do, but I was well aware of the importance of showing total respect for the Eucharist and making sure the host was consumed. I reached into the drawer and gave Mike the Bread from Heaven. We said some prayers, and I could see firsthand the importance of my visit. I am still amazed that I happened to open that drawer, as if a spiritual Eucharistic candle had shone down to get my attention.

Friendship and Prayer

This special visit with the Eucharist opened the door for a deeper level of friendship. Mike's tracheotomy limited our communication to him using his speech board/computer and mouthing words. After a while, that capability was also robbed from him. While ALS showed Mike's body no mercy, given his limitations, we developed a spiritual friendship that centered around prayer and merciful deeds. One devotion that gave us both encouragement was the Chaplet of Divine Mercy; its words united us in prayer and gave my children a thread of hope for Mike. Through this prayer, both my children and I came to understand that while we could not offer him a cure to his disease, we could offer him a prayer that invoked the very ocean of mercy upon his soul. The young children had a difficult time understanding why Mike had to suffer, and yet when we focused on God's mercy, even the experience of suffering became a huge blessing for all of us. Whether we were praying physically together or apart, the Chaplet of Divine Mercy spiritually united and strengthened us.

In the beginning, my goal in this friendship was simply to perform merciful deeds for Mike, in an attempt to follow the formula for mercy mentioned above; doing deeds, speaking words, and offering prayers for others. While these kind deeds may have been the original basis of the relationship, something more was taking place: Good works rooted in love of Jesus are designed to change our hearts. Over the course of our friendship, my heart softened, and my ability to be more compassionate grew. I was no longer looking to perform a good deed out of sympathy; instead, I was able to empathize with him, and I desired to do everything I could in order to alleviate his suffering. What I have slowly come to appreciate about practicing the works of mercy is that in doing so, the focus naturally becomes less about the one serving and more about the good of the person being served. In this way, the works of mercy help to foster in us a more sacrificial, Christ-like love. When we offer deeds, words, and prayers for others, we can bring love to another human being who is yearning for it — even if they don't know it! A life of service softens our hearts and develops our capacity for compassion.

Prayers for the Sick and Dying

In life, little moments of spiritual significance often reveal their value long after the events have taken place. I still recall the day I brought along my dear friend, Shannon, a physical therapist by trade and a fantastic Catholic prayer warrior, to spend time with Mike and to help his body and spirit. For years, I had been telling her about him. Since she lived so close to his care center, she had agreed to pop over and say "hello" from time to time, as well as to offer him physical therapy to help relieve his pain, since his insurance company had stopped covering his physical therapy otherwise.

As we all entered the room that day, we passed Mike's roommate, Patrick, who looked very sick. His eyes were closed, but we could see that one side of his face drooped noticeably, as if he had had a stroke. His appearance startled my children. They often had a hard time processing many of the sights and smells of the nursing home, but each time they visited, they valued the experience, despite any difficulties. Seeing Patrick, though, was a new challenge for them.

I don't remember who suggested that we pray for Patrick, but within an instant we were gathered around Patrick's bed to offer a Chaplet of Divine Mercy. I felt God's presence in a unique way that day as we gathered around this man, who looked so deprived of attention and care, and yet, in God's providence, we were there for him. What a miracle: A mother and her six children, my dear friend (also the mother of a large family), and a stranger gathered to pray, simply because someone on the other side of town introduced me to an unlikely friend. God's providence is truly amazing!

Our prayers that day were marked with a deep feeling of concern for this mystery man. Who was he? Was he a Catholic (or even a Christian)? How did he end up here in this nursing home? I knew one thing with certainty: The Divine Mercy Chaplet was the devotion for him. As the Chaplet continued for about 10 minutes, we all interceded with real concern for this man about whom we knew nothing but his name.

"For the sake of His sorrowful Passion," I focused on the final words on each bead, "have mercy on us and the whole world."

"Us": He was now part of my "us" as we gathered together in prayer in that old institution that had little to offer but systematic care, but we all experienced Christ in our own particular way. It was a beautiful gift to offer Patrick our prayers. As part of the introductory prayers of the chaplet, we prayed the words from St. Faustina's *Diary*: "You expired, Jesus, but the source of life gushed forth for souls, and the ocean of mercy opened up for the whole world" (*Diary*, 1319). We desired that this mystery man would encounter this ocean.

Although my visits to Mike were oftentimes sporadic, for some reason, I returned to visit him the following week. This experience was not typical, and ultimately I believe it was providential. When I walked into the room, I noticed Patrick's bed was empty for the first time ever.

"Where is your roommate?" I asked.

"HE DIED SHORTLY AFTER YOU PRAYED THOSE PRAYERS," Mike typed out on his communication board.

My eyes welled up with tears, and I knew in that moment that Christ had orchestrated a powerful moment, and we were blessed to be part of it.

Mike then added, "NO ONE HAD VISITED PATRICK IN THE FOUR YEARS HE HAD BEEN HERE."

Our small gesture of love was a means of tremendous graces for our mystery friend. In the *Diary*, St. Faustina speaks several times about the graces of praying for the dying:

> I heard these words: "**At the hour of their death, I defend as My own glory every soul that will say this chaplet; or when others say it for a dying**

person, the pardon is the same. When this chaplet is said by the bedside of a dying person, God's anger is placated, unfathomable mercy envelops the soul, and the very depths of My tender mercy are moved for the sake of the sorrowful Passion of My Son" (*Diary*, 811).

Oh, dying souls are in such great need of prayer! O Jesus, inspire souls to pray often for the dying. (Diary, 1015)

[Jesus said:] **"My daughter, encourage souls to say the chaplet which I have given to you. It pleases Me to grant everything they ask of Me by saying the chaplet. ... Write that when they say this chaplet in the presence of the dying, I will stand between My Father and the dying person, not as the just Judge but as the merciful Savior"** (*Diary*, 1541).

[T]he Lord said to me, **"My daughter, help Me to save a certain dying sinner. Say the chaplet that I have taught you for him."** When I began to say the chaplet, I saw the man dying in the midst of terrible torment and struggle. His Guardian Angel was defending him, but he was, as it were, powerless against the enormity of the soul's misery. A multitude of devils was waiting for the soul. But while I was saying the chaplet, I saw Jesus just as He is depicted in the image. The rays which issued from Jesus' Heart enveloped the sick man, and the powers of darkness fled in panic. The sick man peacefully breathed his last. When I came to myself, I understood how very important the chaplet was for the dying. It appeases the anger of God (*Diary*, 1565).

[Jesus said:] **"Pray as much as you can for the dying. By your entreaties, obtain for them trust in My mercy, because they have most need of trust, and have it the least. Be assured that the grace of eternal salvation for certain souls**

in their final moments depends on your prayer. You know the whole abyss of My mercy, so draw upon it for yourself and especially for poor sinners. Sooner would heaven and earth turn into nothingness than would My mercy not embrace a trusting soul" (*Diary*, 1777).

One life lesson that was burned into my heart after praying with Patrick was to make sure to take time to pray with those who are sick, and especially those who are dying. When we take time out of our busy lives in order to be ambassadors of mercy, we can be an instrument of God's mercy to souls.

Long before the Internet or even modern communication, St. Faustina shared with us that our prayers can impact another soul, even when they are far away! The following experiences recorded in her *Diary* make it clear that one does not have to be at the bedside physically. She wrote:

It sometimes happens that the dying person is in the second or third building away, yet for the spirit, space does not exist. It sometimes happens that I know about a death occurring several hundred kilometers away. This has happened several times with regard to my family and relatives and also sisters in religion, and even souls whom I have not known during their lifetime (*Diary*, 835).

No matter who needs prayers, we need to invoke Christ's mercy and learn to trust God with our intentions and our loved ones. Now when I view my Facebook or Instagram social media accounts, I try to remember to pray for these individuals, especially when they post that they are going through a difficult time.

When we offer a heartfelt prayer for those who are breaths away from eternal life, we can be instruments of God's peace and mercy. Since Patrick's passing, I now offer to pray the Chaplet of Divine Mercy for any friend, relative, or acquaintance who is suffering, or who has a family member who is sick and in need of extraordinary graces. I have never been turned down, and I've learned how powerful a gift our prayers are to others.

Heavenly Friendship

Mike died at the age of 48, after a 12-year battle with ALS, on August 29, 2015. In God's divine providence, he was often visited by Dominican brothers who spiritually ministered to him, and his funeral was held at my parish, close to his nursing care center. Mike continues to be remembered by his family, friends, and community through the Michael Vollmer Fund, which was set up to assist other Harvard athletes who have ALS or other neurological disorders.

My long friendship with Mike was a blessing that began with a simple request of a friend. I believe St. Faustina brought me to Mike to get a small taste of what it means to live, suffer, die, and learn to trust Christ in every moment of the day. Because of this experience, I have been inspired to implement the formula for mercy given to us by St. Faustina in my everyday life. When we practice the works of mercy in heartfelt deeds, words, and prayer, life becomes more rewarding and meaningful. If we are open to God's divine plan, He can make us His instruments of mercy in the lives of others. Jesus asked St. Faustina to have an inscription placed at the bottom of the Divine Mercy Image: "Jesus, I trust in You." That powerful inscription is the most significant source of hope for anyone facing difficult life moments.

We must not be timid or fearful of living a life that constantly calls upon Divine Mercy. Jesus told St. Faustina, **"My daughter, do not be afraid of what will happen to you. I will give you nothing beyond your strength. You know the power of My grace; let that be enough"** (*Diary*, 1491). Saint Faustina is an extraordinary example of heroic faith who continues to inspire me to holiness in my everyday, ordinary life, and I am humbled to be called to share in this grand plan of promoting God's mercy through a unique friendship with her.

Jesus, I trust in You.

Portions of this chapter were originally published in a book by
Michele Faehnle and Emily Jaminet, *Divine Mercy for Moms:
Sharing the Lessons of St. Faustina* (Notre Dame, IN:
Ave Maria Press, 2015). Used with permission.

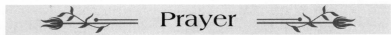

Prayer

A prayer for doing faithfully the holy will of God.

O Jesus, stretched out upon the cross, I implore You,
give me the grace of doing faithfully the most holy will
of Your Father, in all things, always and everywhere. And
when this will of God will seem to me very harsh and
difficult to fulfill, it is then I beg You, Jesus, may power
and strength flow upon me from Your wounds, and may
my lips keep repeating, "Your will be done, O Lord." O
Savior of the world, Lover of man's salvation, who in such
terrible torment and pain forget Yourself to think only of
the salvation of souls, O most compassionate Jesus, grant
me the grace to forget myself that I may live totally for
souls, helping You in the work of salvation, according to
the most holy will of Your Father (*Diary*, 1265).

CHAPTER 3

A Life Intertwined with
My Friend Faustina

Allison Gingras

My introduction to Sr. Maria Faustina of the Most Blessed Sacrament came in 1993, the year she was beatified. At that time, there was a young Polish priest stationed at our parish, who demonstrated his excitement about the upcoming beatification of his fellow countrywoman by adding Sr. Faustina's picture to the church wall. Although fascinated by her unusual habit, it would be years before she would become my saintly friend.

My interest in St. Faustina's powerful message of mercy and trust would not come alive until 2008. My family had made a somewhat painful move to a new parish, but it led to the wonderful blessing of meeting Deacon Gerald (Jerry) Ryan. Deacon Jerry led one of my favorite activities at our new parish home: a Tuesday night Divine Mercy Holy Hour. He would read from St. Faustina's famous *Diary*, offer a thought-provoking reflection, and expose Jesus in the Eucharist on the altar for Adoration. Then we would sing the beautiful Chaplet of Divine Mercy together.

As I heard and read St. Faustina's words, I began to better understand her mission: As it states in the introduction to the *Diary*, "In short, her mission consists in reminding us of the immemorial, but seemingly forgotten, truths of our faith about God's merciful love for men, and in conveying to us new forms of devotion to The Divine Mercy, the practice of which is to lead to the revival of the spiritual life in the spirit of Christian trust and mercy" (*Diary*, Introduction xviii, #2).

At the heart of this mission was the great invitation to trust Jesus, which I struggled with then, and which is still part of my spiritual battle, albeit less so. The more I learned about St. Faustina from her *Diary*, the more I realized how much she and I shared in common. I would like to share four of the most striking parallels: first, the special blessing of having a spiritual director to help discern and accomplish an import-ant calling in life; second, truly learning to trust God in all His ways; third, finding an intimate relationship with Jesus through Adoration of the Blessed Sacrament; and fourth, giv-ing special attention to the 3 o'clock hour each day.

Someone to Guide My Steps

In 2008, I arrived at St. Thomas Aquinas Parish with a fledg-ling desire to work in the New Evangelization, spreading the Catholic faith. I was well aware that in order to be ready to share the faith, many aspects of my own spiritual life needed to be put in order. By then, I had already been through several spiritual directors: One moved, one was just not a good fit, and one was just too far away. So I began praying in earnest for the Lord to bless me with the perfect one for me.

It turns out that Deacon Jerry would not only be the person who introduced me to St. Faustina and the Chaplet of Divine Mercy, but that he would also go on to become my beloved spiritual director. His admiration for St. Faustina's deep conviction of faith played an important role in our time together. These stories have inspired me to want to be closer to Jesus.

I'll never forget the day that the Holy Spirit inspired me to ask Deacon Jerry if he would consider becoming my spiri-tual director. After Mass one Sunday, I was packing up musical equipment after helping to lead our youth choir. I saw the good deacon out of the corner of my eye at the door of the sacristy. I turned to tell the others I was going to go speak to him, but when I looked back, he was gone. *Lord*, I prayed, *I thought for sure you put him there for me to ask. Have I misunderstood this spiritual nudge? Help me know your will.* Suddenly Deacon Jerry reappeared in the doorway. Excited with the quick answer to my prayer, I rushed to speak with him before he disappeared again. My failure to watch where I was going nearly landed me in the good deacon's arms. As I struggled to collect myself, and still a bit off-balance, I blurted out, "I really need to talk to you about being my spiritual director." Deacon Jerry chuckled at my antics and immediately said, "Yes." Maybe he noticed that I, too, was a little quirky, like his friend St. Faustina.

Jesus told St. Faustina to appreciate the true grace of the gift of a spiritual director because not all who pray for a spiritual guide are granted one:

> [Jesus said:] **"And now I am going to tell you something that is most important for you: Boundless sincerity with your spiritual director. If you do not take advantage of this great grace according to My instructions, I will take him away from you, and then you will be left to yourself; and all the torments, which you know very well, will return to you. It displeases Me that you do not take advantage of the opportunity when you are able to see him and talk with him. Know that it is a great grace on My part when I give a spiritual director to a soul. Many souls ask Me for this, but it is not to all that I grant this grace. From the moment when I gave you this priest as spiritual director, I endowed him with new light so that he might easily know and understand your soul"** (*Diary*, 1561).

Without a doubt, I count Deacon Jerry as one of the greatest gifts bestowed on me by Jesus. He truly understands my heart — especially its weaknesses. He has patiently taught me about the enormous blessings of being obedient to the Lord, trusting in Him, and being compassionate to others.

Saint Faustina Helps Me Through the Adoption of My Daughter, Faith

In 2006, my husband, Kevin, and I started to feel this tug on our hearts to pursue adoption. After time in prayer and discussion, we believed that the Lord was calling us to a foreign, special-needs adoption. When I shared this news with my mother, she recalled that one day I came home from school and declared my desire to adopt, as well as my great desire to be the mother of a child who is deaf. My only explanation for these desires is that the Lord put them there so that I would be prepared to answer "yes" when the time came for us to follow through on the Spirit's nudging and adopt a 3-year-old orphan from China who was deaf. I can't help but think of how the psalmist so beautifully expressed this fulfillment of God-given desires: "Find your delight in the Lord, who will give you your heart's desire" (Ps 37:4).

It was during the three-year span between deciding to adopt from China and finally being united with our daughter, Faith, that I truly developed and broadened my trust in Jesus. Saint Faustina played a major role by interceding for me through this challenging period of my life.

We were matched with our little girl, originally named Wu Feng Hua, in April of 2009, but would not meet her until November of that year. We were initially informed that it would take six to eight weeks before we would be traveling to China to bring her home; however, in reality, the wait was a long and torturous six months. On days too many to count during that time, I needed to put my trust of Jesus into practice — and it often required a herculean effort. Those days were spent begging the Lord for an outpouring of grace in order to stay hopeful and patient. I did not want to distrust His love and mercy — He had already bestowed so many gifts upon me during this process! I found these words from the

Diary applicable to my situation and was especially moved by these words:

> Jesus complained to me in these words, "**Distrust on the part of souls is tearing at My insides. The distrust of a chosen soul causes Me even greater pain; despite My inexhaustible love for them they do not trust Me. Even My death is not enough for them. Woe to the soul that abuses these** [gifts]" (*Diary*, 50).

Deacon Jerry said to me, "If you're going to trust God, then trust God." He wanted me to give more than lip service when I said, "I trust in You," and actually surrender to the plan that God the Father had for my life.

We All Have a Great Mission

Besides the normal trepidations that come with adoption, I also had to overcome my anxiety over traveling to China in order to bring my daughter home. It was in the quiet of Adoration that Jesus was able to speak to my heart. Courage came with prayer. My time with Jesus helped me to overcome my natural tendency of avoiding whatever is scary and to embrace the mission of providing a home to an orphan.

The *Catechism of the Catholic Church* says, "Because Christ himself is present in the sacrament of the altar, he is to be honored with the worship of adoration. 'To visit the Blessed Sacrament is ... a proof of gratitude, an expression of love, and a duty of adoration toward Christ our Lord' [Paul VI, *MF* 66]" (*CCC*, 1418).

In Adoration, my greatest struggles melted away, leaving me a sense of peace. Saint Faustina knew this blessing well:

> I was suffering very much, and it seemed to me I would not be able to make my adoration, but I gathered up all my will power and, although I collapsed in my cell, I paid no attention to what ailed me, for

I had the Passion of Jesus before my eyes. When I entered the chapel, I received an inner understanding of the great reward that God is preparing for us, not only for our good deeds, but also for our sincere desire to perform them. What a great grace of God this is! (*Diary*, 450)

A Profound Moment of Grace

By this time, Adoration of the Most Blessed Sacrament had become a regular staple of my prayer life and one of my favorite ways of receiving grace from God. Grace is the undeserved, freely given gift of the Holy Spirit residing within us, who enables us to seek more profoundly God's desires for our lives.

At the time of Faith's adoption, part of my Eucharistic Holy Hour was during the Hour of Great Mercy, which begins at 3 o'clock. As I prayed for the Lord to have mercy on me, end my long suffering of waiting, and finally bring my daughter home, I felt the Lord gently remind me that not everything is about me. In my heart, I just knew the delay was brought about as an answer to somebody else's desire of the heart. In that moment I realized that once she was here we would have Faith with us forever, but her foster family was preparing for what I am sure was a difficult good-bye. In particular, her foster father was on my heart that day.

The Rest of the Story Revealed

Fast forward to November of 2009. We were finally united with our daughter in China. The social worker provided me with a packet of information collected when she visited Faith at her foster home in China. As I read through the paperwork describing Faith's daily schedule, there was a brief note about her foster family. With one sentence, I knew the Lord had truly spoken to me that day in Adoration so many months before. The social worker wrote about a special bond between Faith and her foster father, including a tender note on how he spoiled her, even allowing her to play with his cell phone. What

a special gift Jesus had provided me in that note, reminding me of the special connection we have with Him in Adoration. Saint Faustina wrote:

> I went before the Blessed Sacrament; and when I immersed myself in a prayer of thanksgiving, I heard these words in my soul: **"My child you are My delight, you are the comfort of My Heart. I grant you as many graces as you can hold. As often as you want to make Me happy, speak to the world about My great and unfathomable mercy"** (*Diary*, 164).

Keeping the Divine Mercy Hour or the Divine Mercy Minute

It was during this heart-wrenching time in my life that I read in the *Diary* about the Hour of Great Mercy:

> [Jesus said,] **"At three o'clock, implore My mercy, especially for sinners; and, if only for a brief moment, immerse yourself in My Passion, particularly in My abandonment at the moment of agony. This is the hour of great mercy for the whole world. I will allow you to enter into My mortal sorrow. In this hour, I will refuse nothing to the soul that makes a request of me in virtue of My Passion"** (*Diary*, 1320).

While the agony of waiting for my child to arrive pales in comparison to suffering for the sins of the world, my heart found comfort in the assurance that my prayers during this most holy hour would evoke extra grace. I immediately set my watch alarm to sound each day at 3 o'clock.

> [Jesus said,] **"I remind you, My daughter, that as often as you hear the clock strike the third hour, immerse yourself completely in My mercy, adoring and glorifying it; invoke its omnipotence**

for the whole world, and particularly for poor
sinners; for at that moment mercy was opened
wide for every soul. In this hour you can obtain
everything for yourself and for others for the
asking; it was the hour of grace for the whole
world — mercy triumphed over justice" (*Diary*,
1572).

Almost 10 years later, that alarm is still set. Some days
I take the time to recite an entire Chaplet of Divine Mercy,
while other days, I have just a minute to thank Jesus for His
salvific work upon the Cross. But either way, I always ask for
His blessing on my day and that He would help me to grow in
trust, hope, and faith.

The answers that I receive from my prayer are always in
accordance with the Father's will, and not necessarily my will,
hence the great need for trust. I know I struggle with my desire
to avoid suffering; I want only the good things for which I
pray to happen, and I have to work actively at remembering
that all that God allows is for my ultimate good. He knows
the big picture reason for the suffering. If God did not spare
Jesus, His only begotten Son, from suffering, why should we
not expect to encounter trials?

The other important lesson I took away from this practice
of acknowledging the 3 o'clock hour came from the following
exchange between Jesus and St. Faustina:

[Jesus said:] "**My daughter, try your best to make
the Stations of the Cross in this hour, provided
that your duties permit it; and if you are not able
to make the Stations of the Cross, then at least
step into the chapel for a moment and adore,
in the Blessed Sacrament, My Heart, which is
full of mercy; and should you be unable to step
into the chapel, immerse yourself in prayer there
where you happen to be, if only for a very brief
instant. I claim veneration for My mercy from
every creature, but above all from you, since it**

is to you that I have given the most profound understanding of this mystery" (*Diary*, 1572).

Jesus says, "Step into the chapel for a moment." I wondered how many times I had missed opportunities to be united with Jesus because I thought I had to give a whole hour or nothing at all. My other misconception was that I had to be in the Adoration chapel or the church for it to "count." Jesus reminds us, through this exhortation to St. Faustina, that if we only have a minute, we should still remember His mercy.

Consolation and a sense of humor

With still a month before we could travel to China and bring Faith home, I decided to get my mind off of things by spending the evening enjoying dinner with a friend, who also happened to be a special education teacher. I discussed my plans to homeschool my daughter along with her two brothers. I wished to keep her home, at least for a little while, to get acclimated to family life. My wise and kind friend knew that teaching a child with hearing loss required special skills that, although I was trained in early childhood education, I did not possess. Gently, she tried to explain that it was important for me to be at least open to looking into a School for the Deaf.

I was so overwhelmed by what I could not provide for my daughter instead of all the wonderful things I could offer her. I went home, weighed down beneath my escalating doubts and insecurities. I sat in her prepared, but empty, bedroom — and cried. I told the Lord that I was the wrong person for this mission. *I can't do any of this*, I sobbed, and went to find my Bible for consolation. Realizing that my Bible was in the room with my sleeping husband, I instead chose to read St. Faustina's *Diary*, which I had left on the coffee table.

I prayed. Then I randomly opened the *Diary* and burst into laughter and tears at the same time. The message to which the Spirit had lead me was exactly what I needed to hear, and it was so on point that the only proper reaction to this experience was tears and laughter.

[Jesus] said, **"My daughter, why are you giving in to thoughts of fear?"** I answered, "O Lord, You know why." And He said, **"Why?"** "This work frightens me. You know that I am incapable of carrying it out." And He said, **"Why?"** "You see very well that I am not in good health, that I have no education, that I have no money, that I am an abyss of misery, that I fear contacts with people. Jesus, I desire only You. You can release me from this." And the Lord said to me, **"My daughter, what you have said is true. You are very miserable, and it pleased Me to carry out this work of mercy precisely through you who are nothing but misery itself. Do not fear; I will not leave you alone. Do whatever you can in this matter; I will accomplish everything that is lacking in you. You know what is within your power to do; do that."** The Lord looked into the depth of my being with great kindness; I thought I would die for joy under that gaze. The Lord disappeared, and joy, strength, and power to act remained in my soul. But I was surprised that the Lord did not want to release me and that he is not changing anything He has once said. And despite all these joys, there is always a shadow of sorrow. I see that love and sorrow go hand in hand (*Diary*, 881).

Each worry St. Faustina expressed regarding her mission was one I shared in my call to become Faith's mother. I lacked the proper education to teach a child with a hearing loss, we had absolutely no money to complete the adoption, and I was miserable waiting for her to come home. Even St. Faustina's fear of contact with people made me chuckle, as I am a severe germophobe. Jesus is love and mercy, but this does not exclude truth, as we see clearly in his response to her, **"My daughter, what you have said is true. You are very miserable"** (*Diary*, 881). As difficult, and humorous, as those words were to hear, the next brought such a rush of relief, I could barely breathe as I read them. **"Do whatever you can in this matter; I will accomplish everything that is lacking in you. You know what is within your power to do; do that"** (*Diary*, 881). There was much I could do, and after picking myself up from this pit of despair, I went forward and did just those things. I wrote a letter inviting friends and family to join in our adoption journey with a donation, and we collected the exact amount needed to present to the orphanage. I continued to pray at 3 o'clock each day, asking for safe travels and peace in the waiting. We were blessed with both.

As for educating my daughter, I did stay open to what was best for her. Faith remained home with her brothers and me for five years. When she was adjusted and my education skills hit their limit, we found her the most amazing School for the Deaf, which she adores. She even shares her 45-minute per day van ride with another little girl her same age, also named Faith. "With God all things are possible" (Mt 19:26).

Faustina My Friend

"There's a Polish proverb that goes: *Z kim sie zadajesz takim się stajesz* — 'You become the one you befriend.'"[9] Just how close a friend of St. Faustina I had become was about to be revealed in the most quirky way possible.

Since the crisis of adoption, my alarm continues to ring at 3 o'clock each day to remind me to immerse myself, even for a moment, in the mercy of Jesus. The one thing I have taken away from my time with Jesus, St. Faustina, and the Divine Mercy Chaplet is that the veil between Heaven and earth is not as thick as one might think. This was never more apparent than during a visit to our parish by Fr. Carlos Martins, CC, and the "Treasures of the Church" exhibit of relics.

The evening began with a beautiful presentation by Fr. Martins, which prepares those about to embark on the veneration of over 150 relics, including those of St. Maria Goretti, St. Thérèse of Lisieux (the "Little Flower"), St. Francis of Assisi, St. Thomas Aquinas, and — you guessed it — St. Faustina.

Before we left the church for the display in the parish hall, Fr. Martins said that one or more of the saints we are about to encounter and venerate will want to be "our friend." He clarified that he had no idea how they would make themselves known to us, but that he had seen it happen many times over his years of traveling with the relics, and to rest assured that it would happen for us, too.

My friend Kathy and I entered the main hall in the parish center and excitedly began our veneration of the relics. We went up and down the tables, repeating the same blessing procedure: I would pick up a reliquary, make the Sign of the Cross with it across my body, touch it to the crucifix and Miraculous Medal attached to my necklace, gently put the relic back down, and move onto the next saint. I continued this pattern for over an hour until I reached my favorite nun from Poland, my friend Sr. Maria Faustina of the Blessed Sacrament.

I picked up the relic of the sweet saint who had been listening to my prayers, almost daily, for many years now. She had played an important role in my spiritual and family life journey. I blessed myself — Father, Son, and Holy Spirit — and touched the reliquary glass to my Trinity cross crucifix. As I went to put the reliquary down, I realized my necklace had become completely entangled with this little mini monstrance. I was stuck.

My friend Kathy was stifling a fit of laughter while trying to take my picture, as I begged her to put away her phone and get me free! (In hindsight, I do regret there are no pictures of this hysterical moment with Faustina.) I was starting to draw unwanted attention, and aside from breaking Fr. Martins' rules and leaving with her, I had no option other than to be untwined.

People were all around us prayerfully trying to seek saintly intercession, and here I was entangled with one, stifling (not very well, I might add) my laughter, having a special moment with my friend, St. Faustina. These antics were not really surprising to me; in fact, they seemed right in character: "According to Mrs. Sadowska, Helen [St. Faustina] was always devout, prayerful, and a regular participant in the services in the cathedral. But she also noted that Helen was of such good humor and so witty that she easily could have become a professional comedienne. Her goodness, helpfulness and joyous laughter made her a very lovable person."[10]

Honestly, I'm so grateful she reached out to me so that I would know that she was as fond of me as I was of her. That is the beauty of saintly friendships: They are mutual. Rest assured, the relationship is not just us constantly begging for their help; they are pleased to be our prayer partners, to be our ambassadors to Christ — to be our friends on this journey of faith.

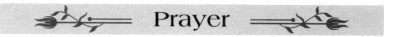

Prayer

Saint Faustina's litany to the Blessed Host.

O Blessed Host, in whom is contained the testament of God's mercy for us, and especially for poor sinners.

O Blessed Host, in whom is contained the Body and Blood of the Lord Jesus as proof of infinite mercy for us, and especially for poor sinners.

O Blessed Host, in whom is contained life eternal and of infinite mercy, dispensed in abundance to us and especially to poor sinners.

O Blessed Host, in whom is contained the mercy of the Father, the Son, and the Holy Spirit toward us, and especially toward poor sinners.

O Blessed Host, in whom is contained the infinite price of mercy which will compensate for all our debts, and especially those of poor sinners.

O Blessed Host, in whom is contained the fountain of living water which springs from infinite mercy for us, and especially for poor sinners.

O Blessed Host, in whom is contained the fire of purest love which blazes forth from the bosom of the Eternal Father, as from an abyss of infinite mercy for us, and especially for poor sinners.

O Blessed Host, in whom is contained the medicine for all our infirmities, flowing from infinite mercy, as from a fount, for us and especially for poor sinners.

O Blessed Host, in whom is contained the union between God and us through His infinite mercy for us, and especially for poor sinners.

O Blessed Host, in whom are contained all the sentiments of the most sweet Heart of Jesus toward us, and especially poor sinners.

O Blessed Host, our only hope in all the sufferings and adversities of life.

O Blessed Host, our only hope in the midst of darkness and of storms within and without.

O Blessed Host, our only hope in life and at the hour of our death.

O Blessed Host, our only hope in the midst of adversities and floods of despair.

O Blessed Host, our only hope in the midst of falsehood and treason.

O Blessed Host, our only hope in the midst of the darkness and godlessness which inundate the earth.

O Blessed Host, our only hope in the longing and pain in which no one will understand us.

O Blessed Host, our only hope in the toil and monotony of everyday life.

O Blessed Host, our only hope amid the ruin of our hopes and endeavors.

O Blessed Host, our only hope in the midst of the ravages of the enemy and the efforts of hell.

O Blessed Host, I trust in You when the burdens are beyond my strength and I find my efforts are fruitless.

O Blessed Host, I trust in You when storms toss my heart about and my fearful spirit tends to despair.

O Blessed Host, I trust in You when my heart is about to tremble and mortal sweat moistens my brow.

O Blessed Host, I trust in You when everything conspires against me and black despair creeps into my soul.

O Blessed Host, I trust in You when my eyes will begin to grow dim to all temporal things and, for the first time, my spirit will behold the unknown worlds.

O Blessed Host, I trust in You when my tasks will be beyond my strength and adversity will become my daily lot.

O Blessed Host I trust in You when the practice of virtue will appear difficult for me and my nature will grow rebellious.

O Blessed Host, I trust in You when hostile blows will be aimed against me.

O Blessed Host, I trust in You when my toils and efforts will be misjudged by others.

O Blessed Host, I trust in You when Your judgments will resound over me; it is then that I will trust in the sea of Your mercy.

Most Holy Trinity, I trust in Your infinite mercy. God is my Father and so I, His child, have every claim to His divine Heart; and the greater the darkness, the more complete our trust should be. (*Diary*, 356-357)

CHAPTER 4

My Miracle of Mercy

Elizabeth Ficocelli

Saint Faustina is one of the best-known saints of modern times. Even young Catholic school children are familiar with the Divine Mercy Chaplet. But in 1993, when this humble Polish nun was beatified, she was hardly a household name — at least not in the United States.

It was about this time when someone handed me a copy of *Diary of Saint Maria Faustina Kowalska: Divine Mercy in My Soul.* I was a new Catholic at the time, and I was intrigued at the concept of apparitions and heavenly messages. If the Church was recognizing someone who had visions of Jesus Christ and transcribed His messages to paper, it was something I certainly wanted to read.

I was quickly engrossed in the *Diary* and the astonishing messages of mercy that Jesus conveyed to Faustina during her years as a religious. My heart burned as I read our Savior's words to His chosen daughter of how He wished to pour out His Divine Mercy on the entire world. I was convinced that these messages were meant in a special way for people of our times — a time when many in the world appear lost, in pursuit of their own way, and devoid of God.

In page after page of the *Diary*, Jesus was pleading for the world to return to Him, the unfathomable font of mercy, to be healed and renewed. No matter what the sin, or more importantly, how *great* the sin, He was offering us a clean start — the ultimate do-over.

It was easy to see why God must have inspired Faustina's confessor, Fr. Michael Sopocko, to encourage the young nun to do what Jesus instructed her, and to document what she was seeing and hearing in writing, though Faustina had less than a third grade education. Her 600-page diary would become a beloved treasure read by millions around the world and, as some theologians have said, one of the most important spiritual writings of all time.

I know that for me, the message of Divine Mercy set a fire deep within. In accord with the *Diary*, I placed a small Image of Divine Mercy on my desk, I prayed the special prayer Jesus taught Faustina for nine consecutive days, and I was anticipating going to Confession the Sunday after Easter for the full remission of sin and punishment (a promise Jesus had made to Faustina). Even though the official Feast of Divine Mercy had not yet been established in the universal Church in those days, I felt it was a grace too important to miss, so I made sure I marked the first Sunday after Easter on my calendar to celebrate God's gift of mercy.

I wanted to tell *everyone* about the message of Divine Mercy, starting with my faith-sharing group. So I took careful notes from the *Diary*, found a short video on Divine Mercy at a local Catholic bookstore, and purchased some holy cards with the Image of Divine Mercy to distribute to the other young adult couples in the group. My hope was that they, too, would find the message of Divine Mercy as life-changing as I had. Little did I know that God and Faustina had much bigger plans for me; that I would one day be sharing about Divine Mercy and trust in God with a far larger audience than my faith-sharing group. But God in His great wisdom knew that in order to do that, I would first have to experience His mercy in a powerful way myself.

Confessions of a Catholic Convert

As I reflect back on those early years as a Catholic, when I first encountered Faustina and the Divine Mercy, I find it ironic that I was so attracted to this message of God's unconditional forgiveness when at the same time I had been struggling for years with the concept of the Sacrament of Confession. As a convert, this Sacrament was terrifying for me. I would force myself to go once or twice a year to meet my obligation, but I always found it to be a miserable, foot-dragging experience. I deplored the idea of going into one of those dark little closets with some man in a collar to tell him all about my failures and humiliations. I was convinced that my pastor would be disappointed if he knew the "real me," so I avoided making my Confession at my own parish at all costs. I was under the delusion that priests kept a "little black book" of everyone's sins, and worse, that they shared Confession stories with other priests over coffee or out on the golf course. Therefore, I would go out of my way to find a parish on the other side of town where I was not known, so that I could make my Confession anonymously.

In truth, however, I was missing out on the meaning and beauty of the Sacrament. I didn't understand that this was an encounter with the living God Himself, as are all of the Sacraments. I wasn't open to receiving what Jesus wanted so desperately to shower upon me — complete, unconditional, transforming mercy. Instead, I would leave the confessional the same way I went in — burdened by my failures and unworthiness.

Maybe it was the words of Jesus on the pages of Faustina's *Diary* that began to make inroads into my hardened heart. Words like, **"My daughter, just as you prepare in My presence, so also you make your confession before Me. The person of the priest is, for Me, only a screen. Never analyze what sort of a priest it is that I am making use of; open your soul in confession as you would to Me, and I will fill it with My light"** (*Diary*, 1725). In any case, it was a necessary precursor to what would unfold.

In the midst of Holy Week that year, with my head and heart filled with the messages of mercy, life took an unexpected turn. For several weeks prior, I had been sleep-deprived; my newborn infant refused to sleep at night, and my patience had long worn out. One particular morning, when my 4-year-old was being stubborn about getting ready for preschool, all the pent-up frustration and impatience came bursting out like a spewing volcano. When I finally pulled myself together, I was completely shocked and devastated at what I had done. I felt like the worst mother in the whole world. Immediately, I knew I had to rectify things: First, I needed to make it better with my son, who was quite shaken by the event. Next, I had to call my husband who was away on a business trip and admit what I had done. It was the worst phone call I've ever had to make. But what I realized I most needed to do was to make this better with God, and there was only one way to do it — Confession.

As an extra self-imposed penance, I swallowed my pride and went to my own parish to confess to my pastor. Nauseated, I drove myself and my infant to the church and walked in. My pulse quickened and I began to sweat as the line for Confession inched forward. I even remember an elderly Italian woman coming up to me in line and offering to hold my baby while I went into the confessional. I didn't even know the woman, but I robotically handed him over, convinced I didn't deserve to have *any* child at that moment. And then it was my turn to enter the confessional.

As my pastor patiently listened, I confessed the whole story between big and ugly sobs. I relayed all the details and how absolutely ashamed I felt. The pastor gave me a few words of advice and then moved on to absolution, almost as if he hadn't heard what I just shared. I sat there on that little wooden chair, waiting for a punishment, a lecture, a dunce cap, or *something*, but it did not come. Confession was over and it was time to leave. Dazed and still wracked with guilt and humiliation, it felt as though the weight of the world pressed down upon my shoulders. I was still filled with self-loathing and unforgiveness toward myself, and it took every bit of energy for me to rise from that chair. And that's when a most amazing miracle — a miracle of mercy — happened.

As I was exiting the confessional, it felt as though someone had placed a bucket of warm water on the threshold above the doorway. As I crossed the threshold, I felt a physical sensation of water splashing over me, washing me clean. In a split second, I felt this incredible sense of joy, peace, and *lightness*, almost as though I were floating. It was such an instantaneous, unexpected, and radical transformation that I knew this had to be from God. It was as though He were acknowledging how contrite I had been over my sin and how happy He was to welcome me back. This, He wanted me to know, was what His genuine healing and forgiveness — His *mercy* — felt like. I recalled the words Jesus imparted to Faustina: "**I pour out a whole ocean of graces upon those souls who approach the Fount of my Mercy. ... [A]ll the divine floodgates through which graces flow are opened**" (*Diary*, 699).

That day, for reasons I cannot explain, I was privileged to receive an undeserved, tangible experience of the power of God's love and mercy. This experience made Faustina's words come alive in a deeper and more meaningful way and it forever changed my attitude about Confession. It gave me great hope that I could be forgiven and start over, like a slate washed clean. God's ocean of mercy was big enough to do that, and it was there just for the asking.

Although I haven't experienced the same tangible sensation since the day of that great miracle, I know that every time I make a sincere Confession in which I am honest about my sinfulness and firmly resolve to try harder with the help of Divine Grace, I am washed clean by God's mercy and invited to start over. Every time *any of us* approach the Lord of Forgiveness in that manner, we receive that great gift and the promise of a new start. This special experience has liberated me from my negative thoughts about the Sacrament of Reconciliation. I no longer drag my feet before I go to Confession. It's not that Confession is easy. But the feelings of forgiveness and freedom are more than worth it. The important thing is, I know now with confidence who it is that awaits me in that confessional; it is Jesus with His arms open, eager to give me His forgiveness and unconditional love despite my failings.

It wasn't long after my "miracle of mercy" that I realized I had been given a great gift — one that I could not hoard for myself. So I decided to take a risk and share the story in an article called "Confessions of a Catholic Convert."[11] Almost immediately after the article was published, a woman contacted me to thank me for my vulnerability. She had always struggled with the Sacrament of Reconciliation, but reading the article gave her the courage to go back after 20 years of being away. I began to receive similar feedback, and I recognized the hand of God at work. Only He could take such a dark situation in my life and use it to bring light to others.

Since that article, I've spoken on what I refer to as the *joy* of Reconciliation to audiences of all ages. For example, I've spoken to small children preparing to receive this Sacrament for the first time. They are naturally filled with curiosity, but also a lot of anxiety. When the students hear the way God allowed me to "feel" his mercy that day, they are able to approach the Sacrament more confidently, eager to receive God's mercy.

At presentations for adult audiences, the results are even more striking. I once shared the story of Faustina and my miracle of mercy as part of a women's retreat in northern Ohio. Before the closing Mass, there was an opportunity for the women to receive the Sacrament of Reconciliation. There were so many women in line for Confession that day that a retired bishop was brought in to help hear them all. These women heard the invitation of Jesus Himself, gently calling them to release to Him the burdens they had been carrying in their hearts (some for many years) that they had been afraid to let go. As I was leaving the closing Mass, the pastor grabbed me by the arm excitedly and whispered in my ear that one of the women he had met with that afternoon had been away from the Sacrament for *40 years.*

Even more amazing, during a parish mission I gave recently, I learned about a woman who came back to the Sacrament after *60 years* of being away. Evidently, she had not been to Confession since her first time at the age of 8. In her recollection, the priest that day was a rather stern, elderly man and most of the children came out of the confessional crying. It was so traumatizing for her that she never returned. But that night, as she listened to my story and what I had learned from Faustina about God's desire to give us a new beginning through Confession, her heart was moved to meet with one of the priests on hand that night. She came out of the confessional radiant, and she has been joyfully making regular Confessions ever since.

When I hear stories like that, my heart is filled with hope that with God all things are possible. Healed hearts, changed lives, new beginnings, the discovery of joy — all of this can happen when we put our trust in Jesus and His unfathomable love and mercy. As difficult as it was for me to walk through my particular trial, I will be forever grateful for the grace and lessons it taught me and how this incident would be used to help others place their hope and trust in God's gift of mercy.

On a hopeful note

Faustina is one of my saintly journey partners or "spiritual girlfriends" as I like to call them. As such, she is someone I can turn to for wisdom and encouragement and comfort. I can invoke her powerful intercession for the trials of life and draw from the precious words of Jesus she captured in her *Diary* to help me know and love the Lord more deeply.

It was Faustina who introduced me to God's unfathomable mercy. She taught me what it means to trust God, and how beautiful results happen in the end when you do. She continues to be there for me every time life demands that I trust in Jesus (which is quite often) and I use her example of steadfast hope to remind me that God is in charge and knows what He is doing at all times.

What impresses me most is the hope that Faustina retained, even in her darkest night, that God would not abandon her. Through her, I have come to see that God uses all situations in life, both good and bad, to accomplish His plans. I have also learned how hope is the strongest weapon against Satan. The evil one tempted Faustina as he tempts us with discouragement, one of his chief weapons in those actively growing in holiness, to make us less effective warriors and prevent us from doing God's work. But Faustina each time clung to God, whom she fully trusted, and Satan was rendered powerless. When I am feeling discouraged and tempted to despair, I ask Faustina for her intercession. I know that just uttering the words, "Jesus, I trust in You," even when I don't genuinely feel it, can cause the devil to flee. Satan's weapon may be discouragement, but ours is hope, and that is always the stronger weapon.

Jesus, I trust in You!

Portions of this story were originally published in *Therese, Faustina and Bernadette: Three Saints who Challenged My Faith, Gave Me Hope and Taught Me How to Love* by Elizabeth Ficocelli (Notre Dame, IN: Ave Maria Press, 2014). Used with permission.

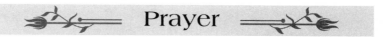

Prayer

Saint Faustina's prayer to hidden Jesus.

Hidden Jesus, life of my soul,
Object of my ardent desire,
Nothing will stifle Your love in my heart.
The power of our mutual love assures me of that.

Hidden Jesus, glorious pledge of my resurrection,
All my life is concentrated in You.

It is You, O Host, who empower me to love forever,
And I know that You will love me as Your child in
return.

Hidden Jesus, my purest love,
My life with You has begun already here on earth,
And it will become fully manifest in the eternity to come,
Because our mutual love will never change.

Hidden Jesus, sole desire of my soul,
You alone are to me more than the delights of heaven.
My soul searches for You only, who are above all gifts
and graces, You who come to me under the form of
bread.

Hidden Jesus, take at last to Yourself my thirsting heart
Which burns for You with the pure fire of the Seraphim.
I go through life in Your footsteps, invincible,
With head held high, like a knight, feeble maid though
I be. (*Diary*, 1427)

CHAPTER 5

My Soul Sister Faustina

Brooke Taylor

Standing with my newly adopted baby daughter at Jasna Góra Monastery in Czestochowa, Poland, I stepped in line to venerate the relics of St. Faustina, St. Maximilian Kolbe, and St. John Paul the Great. The procession of people wrapped behind the altar of the Black Madonna, waiting to touch the relics. My heart raced as I considered the enormity of the occasion. Here in the presence of Our Lady of Czestochowa, we were moments away from visiting the saints who had become our very real companions on an unbelievable journey. This pilgrimage with my new little girl was the culmination of a story I would scarcely have believed, had I not personally lived it. As we patiently inched closer to the relics, my mind drifted back to the road that brought us here.

Shortly after our third son was born, we were open to life and the possibility of more children. Month after month we prayed. Months turned into years, and I was diagnosed with secondary infertility. Working as a morning show co-host on a contemporary Christian radio station brought many opportunities to hear adoption testimonies, participate in pro-life rallies, and learn about the needs of waiting children. We had never considered it before, but after witnessing the beauty of adoption, the Holy Spirit opened my heart to the possibility. We began to cautiously discern. We looked at fostering, as well as local and international adoption. At the time, everything just seemed too expensive and complicated.

In May 2009, my husband and I were invited to Washington, D.C., to a movie premiere with former Speaker of the House Newt Gingrich and his wife Callista. They were promoting their film *Nine Days that Changed the World,* a powerful documentary about Pope John Paul II's historic trip to Poland in 1979 and the Holy Father's deep devotion to the Black Madonna. As a revert to the Catholic faith, I had never even heard of the Black Madonna until the movie. I left the film deeply moved and inspired to learn more about the Polish people and Our Lady of Czestochowa. The following week, I shared my experience with the listeners on my podcast, *Good Things Radio,* and through my blog. I told the story of the film and the Black Madonna. Then I noticed an ad on my website that said: "Adopt from Poland." It grabbed my heart. *Poland?* Could this be where the Lord was leading? From that day forward, it was as if we had boarded a roller coaster powered by the Holy Spirit.

My husband and I both felt a strong prompting. We made the call to inquire about adoption from Poland. The proposition would be an expensive one. As a middle-class family with three children, this was terrifying. We were tethered to one another through prayer and trust, navigating hills and hanging on for the next turn with white knuckles. Surely the Lord was not asking us to go into debt. How could we pull this off? In my spirit, I began to hear the question, *Do you have room for me?* My heart was hearing the call of a child. Despite my fears, the answer was "yes." "Jesus, I trust in You" became my perpetual prayer.

During months of paperwork, physicals, background checks, and notarized and postilled papers, we discovered that a few special friends were walking alongside us. We begged the intercession of Pope St. John Paul II. A simple movie premiere about the Holy Father had been the first mark on the map leading us to Poland. I sensed he was in our midst, along with St. Faustina Kowalska. Not knowing much about her except that she had been a Polish nun devoted to Divine Mercy, I set out on a mission to learn more about her life, and I began to read the *Diary* for the first time.

Saint Faustina became a friend through the long months. Her spirituality resonated with me during the sleepless nights when I wondered *where* and *who* our child would be. With my alarm blaring a 2 a.m. wakeup call, St. Faustina inspired me to begin my day at the family kneeler, reading portions of the *Diary* and laying my impatience and longing before the Lord. The more I immersed myself in her words, the deeper my desire grew to spend time in the presence of Jesus enthroned in the Blessed Sacrament. I began to wake even earlier, allowing myself time to stop at the Adoration chapel on my way to the radio station.

Spending time with my friend St. Faustina taught me the value of quiet contemplation. For years, I was always in a hurry. Most days, I'm still in a hurry. I hardly remember a time before multitasking or rushing to the next thing. I have struggled with the belief that unless I am constantly on the go, I am not being productive. Faustina inspired me to see the value of *stopping* to pray. As the creator of "The Sacred Sink" blog, my mission is to pray while cleaning, working, driving, and folding laundry. Faustina likewise sought to maintain communion with our Lord in work and play, but I noticed it was during silent Adoration that she was free to stop and listen wholly. Following St. Faustina's example taught me the profound value of the slow work of God. I found that during the many months of waiting, the more I sat with my Beloved, the more my need for control diminished. The pre-dawn visits to the Adoration chapel gave me endurance and peace. I could relate to the longing and love of St. Faustina for Jesus. This provided much needed sacred stamina for the journey.

As the months wore on, it became clear that more was coming. Our lives were about to get much more intense. My dad was diagnosed with small cell lung cancer. The prognosis was bleak. We also learned the shocking news that after four years of infertility, I was pregnant! With fear that our adoption would be derailed because of my pregnancy, I ran to my friends, St. Faustina, St. John Paul II, St. Maximilian Kolbe, and Our Lady of Czestochowa. I begged their intercession. Adoptions can be filled with legal minefields and complexities that often take years to sort out. I was overjoyed about my pregnancy, but I also knew it could impact the adoption process. If my baby was born before we received our referral, it would disqualify our current application status. It would require us to start the process all over again, even after we had invested so much time and money. Worry consumed me.

Taking these fears to Jesus in Adoration, I opened my tattered copy of the *Diary* and read these words:

> **"Do as much as is in your power, and don't worry about the rest. These difficulties prove that this work is Mine"** (*Diary*, 1295).
>
> I saw Jesus in a bright garment, near my kneeler. He said, **"Why are you afraid to do My will? Will I not help you as I have done thus far?"** (*Diary*, 489).

Those words are now printed out and taped to my closet wall. Aided by Faustina and trusting in God's word, I revealed the news of my pregnancy to our adoption agency. They promptly *expedited* the process and assured us they would do everything possible to connect us with our waiting child and finalize the adoption before our baby was born! Fundraisers brought much needed help with costs, and friends and strangers generously gave donations and prayers. Although we had already settled on the name "Mary Grace," if our child was a girl, I began to notice something unexpected.

In prayer, while driving, or even while on the treadmill, the name "Karolina" would pop into my mind. We had no idea if our baby would be a girl or a boy at this point, but I just couldn't shake the name Karolina. Things like this didn't normally happen to me. I never imagined I was special enough or holy enough for the Lord to speak to me. Before this chapter of my life, I likely would have dismissed it. But I had become so familiar with the *Diary* that I knew it *was possible* for God to break through my thoughts and implant a message and a name, even to insignificant me! As a believer, I had always marveled at how God spoke to His people — in the burning bush, in the cloud by day, in audible commands to Samuel, Zechariah, and the great prophets. As a student of the saints and lover of their biographies, I knew our Lord continued to communicate with His holy ones throughout the ages, like St. Joan of Arc, St. Bernadette Soubirous, and so many others. But it wasn't until I had immersed myself in Faustina's world that I even considered myself worthy to hear from God so directly. Her humble obedience and unfiltered love showed me that God's merciful gaze is fixed on all of us, but it is we who so often fail to gaze back at Him and hear His messages.

On March 5, 2010, I ran into a Polish friend at church. I shared our latest update with her, including my periodic visions of the name Karolina. "Is the name Polish?" I asked. "Oh, yes! It's very Polish, it's actually quite common," she said. That evening, we received word from our agency that they had our referral. Our child was now ready for a family. "A special little girl," they told us. A *girl*! With trembling hands, I put the phone on speaker. My husband and I locked tear-filled eyes and held our breath for more information. Our adoption agent told us a few details: She was born six weeks premature; she was 8 months old with blonde hair and green eyes ... *"And her name is Karolina."*

Karolina was the name that was given to her in the hospital by the orphanage director. The name the Lord had given her. The name He had revealed to us. The feminine version of Karol. The birth name of Karol Wotiyla, who later became Pope John Paul II.

> **"And I thought of you before I called you into being"** (*Diary*, 1292).
> **Fear not, for I have redeemed you; I have called you by name: you are mine (Is 43:1).**

We also learned that her orphanage was in Czestochowa, Poland, the home of Jasna Gora Monastery and the Black Madonna. Exactly where our journey to Karolina first began. "Oh, how great is your beauty, Jesus my Spouse! Living

Flower enclosing life-giving dew for a thirsting soul! My soul is drowned in You" (*Diary*, 501).

As Karolina and I approached the relics behind the Black Madonna that day, I reflected on all of this. Astonished and grateful, I touched her chubby 11-month-old hand to the relics of St. Faustina, St. Maximilian Kolbe, and St. John Paul the Great. In that moment I felt a rush of heat, and a sense of acute clarity that I needed to be prepared. My heart braced myself for what my mind did not yet know. It is impossible to explain the arc of spiritual electricity that burned through me. I understood a cross would be imminent, but an absolute peace filled my spirit. This was especially branded in my mind because the sensation was coming through *Karolina's* hand, since she was the one touching the relics directly. Jesus' words to Faustina were again appropriate: **"My daughter, do not be afraid of sufferings: I am with you"** (*Diary*, 151).

The spiritual quickening I received that day was indeed a divine message of preparation. The years have been fraught with challenges. Shortly after we returned from Poland, we received the word that my father was terminal. I realized that after our adoption we would not simply ride off into a "happily ever after" sunset. Life would go on with grief, hardships, joy, and grace.

We would receive roses: Our surprise pregnancy resulted in a healthy, beautiful son, Augustine Lawrence, named after my father; friends and family who had prayed for so long would welcome our daughter lovingly into a community of unconditional love; and our three older boys would tenderly guide their sister with patience and affection.

We also experienced thorns: The ravages of cancer were ceaseless; my daughter was diagnosed with severe, institutional autism and global developmental delays; and I was physically and emotionally drained, overwhelmed with chronic fatigue.

Yet even in the darkness, there was a current of peace that flowed through our family. The words from the *Diary* of St. Faustina continued to speak to me: "Only love has meaning; it raises up our smallest actions into infinity" (*Diary*, 502).

During times of desolation, impatience, and fear, the words of St. Faustina gave me reason to hope. "Jesus, I trust in you" were among the only words I could pray during my father's last days in hospice.

During times of joy the message of St. Faustina's *Diary* reminded me that Jesus pursues us and delights in our happiness. **"Know that as often as you come to Me, humbling yourself and asking My forgiveness, I pour out a super-abundance of graces on your soul, and your imperfection vanishes before My eyes, and I see only your love and your humility"** (*Diary*, 1293). During times of spiritual dryness, physically exhausted and depleted of all energy, Faustina's zeal renewed my fervor. "My Jesus, support me when difficult and stormy days come, days of testing, days of ordeal ... . Sustain me, Jesus, and give me strength to bear suffering. Set a guard upon my lips that they may address no word of complaint to creatures. Your most merciful Heart is all my hope" (*Diary*, 1065).

Another enduring quality of St. Faustina's that I so greatly admire was her absolute attentiveness to the Lord. She had already taught me the art of slowing down and embracing time in Adoration. Likewise, she became my novice master in understanding the importance of focus. I smile thinking about how Karolina worked alongside St. Faustina in a mystical way to teach me this lesson.

During Karolina's occupational therapy sessions, the therapist would often remark that Karolina "does not attend well." In other words, she lacks the focus needed to complete a given task. Watching her, I could see how she would focus on everything else but the one thing she was being asked to tend to!

In some cases, the room would be cleared of everything else to "set her up for success" so that nothing else could distract her from the one mission she was being asked to accomplish. It wasn't until the room was devoid of all other distractions that Karolina could truly "monotask" and focus on the assigned work. That observation was a lightbulb moment in my own life. How often do I not "attend well" in my vocation? On any given day, I get lost in distractions, frivolous time-wasters, and worrying about everything else but the given task the Lord is asking me to focus on.

Faustina devoted her life to *attending well*. Her interior thoughts reveal a soul in perpetual union with our Lord. The 3 o'clock hour is a good example of this. During a time that is typically stressful during the school year, as my children rush through the door all at once, Faustina reminds me to "attend" to our Lord and immerse myself in His mercy. A moment to stop what I am doing (this is always hard)! To focus. To pray. It doesn't take long, but this simple act of attending gives me a shot of grace and resets my soul.

> **[A]s often as you hear the clock strike the third hour, immerse yourself completely in My mercy, adoring and glorifying it; invoke its omnipotence for the whole world, and particularly for poor sinners; for at that moment mercy was opened wide for every soul. In this hour you can obtain everything for yourself and for others for the asking; it was the hour of grace for the whole world — mercy triumphed over justice (*Diary*, 1572).**

Jesus called Faustina "Secretary of My mercy" (*Diary*, 965). She was uneducated and limited in her resources, yet she *attended* to her Master and transcribed His every word with astonishing grace, obedience, and humility. On March 21, 1935, she wrote in her *Diary*:

> Often during Mass, I see the Lord in my soul; I feel His presence which pervades my being. I sense His divine gaze; I have long talks with Him without saying a word; I know what His divine Heart desires, and I always do what will please Him the most. I love Him to distraction, and I feel that I am being loved by God. At those times, when I meet

with God deep within myself, I feel so happy that I do not know how to express it. Such moments are short, for the soul could not bear it for long, as separation from the body would be inevitable. Though these moments are very short, their power, however, which is transmitted to the soul, remains with it for a very long time. Without the least effort, I experience the profound recollection which then envelops me — and it does not diminish even if I talk with people, nor does it interfere with the performance of my duties. I feel the constant presence of God without any effort of my soul. I know that I am united with Him as closely as a drop of water is united with the bottomless ocean. (*Diary*, 411)

Starting with our adoption and continuing with our special needs journey with Karolina, my friend Faustina has shown me how to better attend to Jesus in the ordinary events of my life, creating mercy minutes as I live out my vocation as wife and mother. I struggle with the sorrow of wishing my daughter was whole and healed from the heavy crosses she carries every day. I feel the weight of being a caregiver. While it is the greatest honor of my life, I wrestle with constant doubt in myself and my ability to give my daughter all she needs to overcome her many challenges. I cling to Faustina still today, not because I am pious and perfect, but because she reminds me how deeply Jesus loves us and shares our sorrows. How His mercy rescues me when I am in the mire. A simple holy card with the Divine Mercy Image calls me back to Him, to affix my heart to His, allowing the blood and water of His mercy to flow through me. This is my life preserver in times of darkness. Faustina is an everyday companion that brings me closer to Jesus through her example of becoming a "host — or sacrifice" (*Diary*, 485) and emptying herself to be filled by Jesus on the cross. This is a reminder I need constantly. Even in the car, the Divine Mercy Chaplet in song brings a holy hush to a noisy minivan full of kids and dispenses graces amidst the hectic events of the day. This is an ever-present comfort. Through St. Faustina's simple way of *listening* and loving, journaling and prayer, and focusing on the Lord, she became a great mystic and messenger of Divine Mercy.

In his homily at the canonization Mass for St. Faustina (April 30, 2000), Pope St. John Paul II prayed: "Faustina, a gift of God to our time, a gift from the land of Poland to the whole Church, obtain for us an awareness of the depth of Divine Mercy; help us to have a living experience of it and to bear witness to it among our brothers and sisters. ... Today, fixing our gaze with you on the face of the risen Christ, let us make our own your prayer of trusting abandonment and say with firm hope: Christ Jesus, I trust in you!"[12]

Faustina's complete surrender to God's will transformed not only the trajectory of her life, but also her own religious community, and ultimately the world. As a student of mercy, she also became a teacher. Just like any good "big sister," St. Faustina guides me along the way of mercy, lovingly teaching me through her prayers, her love for the Eucharist, and her relationship with Jesus. She took my outstretched hand and led me to the deep waters to have a "living experience" of Divine Mercy. I bear witness to it today through the miracle of my precious daughter. We, after all, are *all* adopted sons and daughters of God, and heirs of His kingdom.

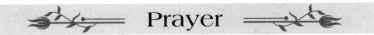

Prayer

Saint Faustina's prayer to
the Blessed Host.

O Blessed Host, in golden chalice enclosed for me,
That through the vast wilderness of exile
I may pass — pure, immaculate, undefiled;
Oh, grant that through the power of Your love
this might come to be.

O Blessed Host, take up Your dwelling within my soul,
O Thou my heart's purest love!
With Your brilliance the darkness dispel.
Refuse not Your grace to a humble heart.

O Blessed Host, enchantment of all heaven,
Though Your beauty be veiled
And captured in a crumb of bread,
Strong faith tears away that veil.
(*Diary*, 159)

CHAPTER 6

Gardens of Mercy

Kaitlyn Mason

There is no doubt in my heart that we are living in a great time of mercy. In 1935, St. Faustina reported in her *Diary* that Jesus told her, "**You will prepare the world for My final coming**" (*Diary*, 429). Sister Lucia of Fatima told us, "The Most Holy Virgin in these last times in which we live has given a new efficacy to the recitation of the Rosary to such an extent that there is no problem, no matter how difficult it is, whether temporal or, above all, spiritual, in the personal life of each one of us, of our families, of the families of the world, or of the religious communities, or even of the life of peoples and nations that cannot be solved by the Rosary."[13] I believe that in our time now, God has given a special efficacy to the life, work, and message of St. Faustina. This book serves as further evidence that God graced St. Faustina with a special task, one she continues to carry out in Heaven, as she has impacted each of our lives. This task is to set the world ablaze with the message and devotion of Divine Mercy, and that is a task I'm happily taking up along with St. Faustina, on this side of Heaven.

It All Started with Mary

It all started when my friend gave me a giant statue of Mary. It was a bright, gloriously painted depiction of Our Lady of Guadalupe (though I must confess I had no idea it was Our Lady of Guadalupe at the time). I was struck by the golden stars painted against deep cobalt blue.

The Catholic faith is deeply rooted in my family heritage. However, Marian devotion was still a mystery to me at this point in life. What would I do with an 18-inch statue of Mary? Wasn't this idolatry or something? *Maybe I could just take her out at Christmastime,* I thought. So, I did what people do when they don't want to think about something anymore. I packed Mary in a box and stuffed her away in a closet. Eventually, I became so uncomfortable with Mary that I gave the statue away to Goodwill.

But I couldn't discard my discomfort. Will Smith once said when "something hurts, lean in," and that's sort of how I handled my Marian discomfort. Since I had never heard of the *Catechism*, I had no idea where to start looking for what the Church really teaches. Being a millennial, I naturally started exploring via Google. I stumbled across the concept of a Mary Garden, and I was fascinated. Christians have planted flowers in honor of Mary for centuries. The morning glory flower is known as "Our Lady's Mantle"; the lily of the valley is "Our Lady's Tears"; the daffodil is "Mary's Star"; and the list goes on. Dozens of flowers bear Marian names, and countless Mary Gardens bloom at churches and homes throughout the world.

I was intrigued, particularly with the beauty and simplicity of these gardens. They seemed to instill a certain sense of community and joy wherever they were planted. The bursting forth of Marian flowers gave hope to an aching world. The more I learned about Marian devotion, the more I became enchanted with the idea of honoring Mary with love just as her Son, Jesus, did. Scott Hahn's book *Hail Holy Queen* would then bring me deeper into the fullness of Marian devotion.

The previous summer, after a powerful experience in Adoration, I knew I was being called to become a mother. When I became pregnant with our first child, I was blessed and honored to receive four baby showers to celebrate our daughter's arrival into the world. We were showered with mercy and love.

During this time, I served as a pregnancy hotline volunteer for our local crisis pregnancy center. They provided me with training that helped prepare me for counseling women in crisis over the phone. I found a stark contrast between my own experiences in pregnancy and those of so many women whom I was counseling. The lack of support they received bothered me immensely. Little did I know, these experiences were also preparing me to share mercy and love with my little sister, who would soon face a crisis pregnancy of her own.

When my mom informed me that my sister was unexpectedly pregnant and desperately in need of counseling and encouragement, I reached out to her immediately. I remember pacing the floor of our daughter's nursery as I spoke to my sister over the phone, hoping and praying she would find the courage she needed to bring her son into the world.

When she ultimately chose to embrace her motherhood, I wanted so badly to be able to share with my sister the joy of a baby shower. My showers served as a sort of rite of passage for me, equipping me with faith and confidence in my budding motherhood. Moreover, every life deserves a celebration. I called multiple churches and pro-life ministries in her area, and no one was willing to help me with the shower. In the end, long distance and family strain made a shower impossible. If I couldn't pull something together for my sister, I would find a way to support other mothers in crisis pregnancy situations.

The Birth of an Apostolate

The Holy Spirit helped me connect the dots, and an idea was conceived for a new apostolate called Mary Garden Showers. We would seek to empower and encourage women in crisis pregnancies through baby showers for women choosing to parent, and blessing showers for women lovingly placing a child for adoption. Ideas for how we could create a cross-country network of showers kept flooding in, and I fervently wrote everything down in a notebook.

Then something happened. I doubted everything. I became convinced that these ideas wouldn't work and that Mary Garden Showers could never become a reality. People wouldn't really support this, would they? How was I supposed to get started on this as a new mother myself? To complicate matters, my family was gearing up to move closer to my parents who lived several states away, which meant I was about to be extremely busy taking care of that process, and I had no idea where we would be going to church in our new town. How could I start a ministry out of nothing in a new place with people I'd never met before? Would I be able to find a priest and parish who would be supportive of celebrating all women and babies in crisis pregnancies? Even mothers who were teenagers? Even mothers who battled addiction? By the time we were packing boxes for our move, our second baby was on the way. How would I ever have time to lead a new ministry with two babies under age 2? So, like St. Faustina who burned her first diary when doubt crept in, I recycled my Mary Garden Showers notebook. It went out of my home in the same clean out effort that sent Mary to Goodwill.

When we moved to Charlotte, North Carolina, I decided to try to bring Mary Garden Showers to life. It quickly became clear that the Holy Spirit was present in this work, and that I needed only to trust. We found a wonderful parish with an incredibly supportive pastor, and we started hosting showers. The community plugged in, lives were touched, babies were born, and we joyfully kept going. We created a manual to make it easy for other churches to join our mission, and our apostolate started to spread across the country. My good friend and co-director Serena Boykin and I quickly realized that while the showers were lovely, we longed for a solid, strong, Catholic message to share with these women in their time of greatest need. We prayed for a message to share.

Connecting with Divine Mercy

Like so many good things in this world, our apostolate was hit hard with difficulties. Meanwhile, I was battling crippling postpartum anxiety after the birth of our second child. During this challenging time, Serena suggested that we pray a novena to Our Lady of Sorrows. This novena was a turning point in my life, one that would ultimately awaken my heart anew to the joy of Christ. I began to experience life in a profoundly new way, and things have never been the same.

Serena was reading the *Diary* of St. Faustina at the time. She gave me her copy as a gift. I pored through several pages and, like so many others, found a great friend and confidante in St. Faustina. This was a woman who truly understood what I was going through. So a friendship began. It was as if St. Faustina came, took my hand, and began to lead me through my doubts, ever closer to Christ and His ocean of mercy. Never before had I experienced a saint as a real, tangible friend in my life.

It was the Jubilee Year of Mercy, and I had come a long way since stuffing Mary in a closet. I was preparing to make my Marian Consecration at the end of Lent on the Feast of the Annunciation. While I longed to bring women in crisis closer to Mary, I still wasn't sure how to grow closer to Mary myself until I found this simple, easy, quick way to Jesus through Mary called Marian Consecration. I began reading *33 Days to Morning Glory* by Fr. Michael Gaitley, MIC. With Lent wrapping up and my book almost finished, I still had some lingering questions about Mary. So I decided to attend a Mercy and Mary retreat in Tennessee at about 36 weeks pregnant. "You know Mary's got a hold of you," one retreat attendee told me, "when she brings you all the way through the mountains at 36 weeks pregnant to a retreat by yourself!" Father Gaitley was really sick on the retreat, but he kept showing up and continued to share with us throughout the weekend. I was blown away by his message and persistent dedication to Divine Mercy. This was the message Mary Garden Showers desperately needed to share. This was our call to action!

So, we took St. Faustina and her message of Divine Mercy into the heart of Mary Garden Showers. Today, the Marian Missionaries of Divine Mercy graciously supply us with canvas Divine Mercy Images that we ship to our chapters throughout the country. Then, we present a canvas to each mother at her own personal shower. It is perhaps my favorite moment of each shower when I get to look into the eyes of a frightened mother and direct her gaze toward the loving gaze of Christ in the Image of Divine Mercy. I explain to her that Jesus Christ loves her and her baby, that there is an ocean of mercy available to her at every moment, and that this image of mercy can serve as a constant reminder to her that she is worthy of the love of God. In the darkness of her crisis situation, whether it is the darkness of addiction, homelessness, depression, anxiety, fear, confusion, neglect, or abuse, Jesus Christ is with her through it all, penetrating and piercing through the darkness with the rays of His infinite mercy.

Mary Garden Showers currently has six active chapters operating in North Carolina, Indiana, Ohio, and Minnesota, with more chapters forming or discerning involvement at this time. There is a great need for this work. People are eager to plug in and assist in pro-life efforts, but often are looking for a tangible way to help. Much different than a behind the scenes supply drive, Mary Garden Showers provides a simple, non-judgmental format for connecting people in need of mercy and love with the heart of the Catholic Church. In this way, a woman can visibly see the Church coming together to celebrate the life of her child. Often, this is the first opportunity the mother has to truly celebrate and be happy about the arrival of her baby.

The women we connect with come from many different backgrounds and faiths, and many are not familiar with Catholicism. We want to encourage them to follow the wonderful example of Mary who, with her *fiat*, chose to love and give life to Jesus. We continue to experience that by loving each mother, she is filled with the love she needs to embrace motherhood and choose birth for her child. Women have turned away from abortion after learning they would be able to receive a loving shower. In this way, just as a gardener encourages more flowers to bloom, Mary Garden Showers encourages more little lives to be brought into this world. We are planting a new kind of garden for Mary.

Divine Mercy in the Heart of My Home

The Mercy and Mary retreat in Tennessee impacted my home life as well. Our homework one night of the retreat was to pray one decade of the Divine Mercy Chaplet. I had never heard this prayer before. Our hotel had a fire pit out back, and there was a group gathering there for prayer. They invited me to join their circle. As I sat there under the stars, I listened and prayed, and slowly, I learned to recite the beautiful prayer that is the Chaplet of Divine Mercy. Later, I would feel Jesus asking me to pray this prayer unceasingly, just as He asked this of St. Faustina. This is a calling for each of us, to keep the words of Christ's mercy ever on our mind, on our lips, and in our hearts. "For the sake of His sorrowful passion, have mercy on us and on the whole world," I whisper as I do the dishes. "For the sake of His sorrowful passion, have mercy on us and on the whole world," I beg as I recall the sins I have committed against others, and that others have committed against me and against God. "For the sake of His sorrowful passion, have mercy on us and on the whole world," my daughters say when we join together in prayer at the hour of mercy. "For the sake of His sorrowful passion, have mercy on us and on the whole world," my husband and I pray as we prepare to bring another child into this big, beautiful world. I try to keep this prayer with me always, that I may become a vessel of mercy more and more with each breath.

After making my Marian Consecration, I felt a strong pull to wear a scapular. I researched the many types and asked Mary for guidance on which one I should wear. That night, a dream made it clear that I was to wear the white scapular of Our Lady of Mercy. In the dream, Mary said, "When there's a war going on, it's the least we can do to take up our cross and fervently pray for those who need it most." As she said the words "take up our Cross," I saw that someone was putting the white scapular over my head. Saint Faustina's order centered on Mary under the title of Our Lady of Mercy, so this scapular serves as another way that I feel drawn to St. Faustina and her work of Divine Mercy.

I attended a second Mercy and Mary retreat at Fr. Chris Alar's home church, which happens to be my parents' church. This time, I took my husband, Benjamin, and my mother. I can't get enough of this message! The rich story of mercy that flows throughout the ages, and in a special way through the 20th century into our present day, truly comprises (as Fr. Michael Gaitley, MIC, suggests in his book of the same name) the second greatest story ever told.

Benjamin was then on fire about Divine Mercy. Together we took St. Faustina and Divine Mercy into the heart of our home. We consecrated our family to Divine Mercy with Fr. Gaitley's book *33 Days to Merciful Love*. Now, there's a page in St. Faustina's *Diary* where she places a big X over the paper, and declares, "From today on, my own will does not exist" (*Diary*, 374). After our consecration to Divine Mercy, we began living this way. This surrender to God's Will and our openness to being a vessel of mercy would swiftly bring our family into a new home and a new way of life.

Ark of Divine Mercy Homestead

Saint Faustina belonged to the Congregation of the Sisters of Our Lady of Mercy in Krakow, Poland. To this day, this order oversees the operation of "mercy houses." At mercy houses, women caught in prostitution or other moral and physical perils find restoration, healing, and hope. This is certainly similar to the work of Mary Garden Showers. It is also similar to a new calling my family is striving to live out each day.

We recently felt called to move from our home owner association-cookie-cutter neighborhood to a few acres of land to create a community-focused, merciful homestead. I might have been more mentally comfortable owning as little as possible, hiding away like hermits in an RV or pop-up camper or something. You know, the trendy minimalism thing. But you can only fit so many guests on those little bunk beds and pop-up tables, and our family continually feels called to a physically larger form of hospitality. We're told in Hebrews, "Do not neglect hospitality, for through it some have unknowingly entertained angels" (Heb 13:2). We're trying to listen.

We affectionately refer to our home as "Ark of Divine Mercy Homestead." First, we entrusted our house to Jesus through an enthronement of the Sacred Heart, formally declaring Jesus Christ king of our home and family. We then asked Jesus and Mary to help us understand God's will for our family and who to bring into our home.

When a new mother called in tears with nowhere to live with her newborn son, we asked her to move in. Her tears of sorrow turned to tears of joy, and that is the work of our Merciful Lord. God also used our open home to provide room and board to a traveling pro-life ministry, to share the message of mercy with others through "Divine Mercy, Dinner, and Dessert" nights in our living room, and to invite others to use our land with us for cooperative family farming.

Saint Faustina answered the door of her convent and assisted with needs of visitors. As a wife and mother, I answer the door to our home, assisting with needs of all who enter. On days when simple home care and hospitality tasks are a struggle, I think of St. Faustina and the potatoes that turned to roses before her eyes. **"I change such hard work of yours into bouquets of beautiful flowers, and their perfume rises up to My throne,"** Jesus said (*Diary*, 65). Perhaps Jesus will be pleased with our attempts to serve, as well. He does not require perfection, but He does want our full effort.

At our Ark of Divine Mercy Homestead, we're attempting to give God our full effort. We feel called to explore a permaculture lifestyle of living closer to the land and community God has blessed us with. We first learned about these agricultural methods through a newsletter from Fr. Michael Gaitley, as permaculture is being put to use near the National Shrine of Divine Mercy in Stockbridge, Massachusetts. We look forward to visiting there one day to grow in devotion to Divine Mercy, to learn more about permaculture, and to join St. Faustina in prayer on this side of Heaven.

While tending to a garden and cooking the harvest were tasks of St. Faustina's, and common tasks for many in her day, the hustle and bustle of society increasingly draws us away from these menial, humble tasks. Yet there is value in working the land with God our Creator to create gardens that nourish both body and soul. Humanity originated in Eden, and with access to God's infinite supply of life-giving Divine Mercy, we can work on earth to bring every soul possible back to the paradise intended for all. We can do this in many ways, one of which is by filling a garden with crops, cooking the harvest, and bringing the community together for the feast.

We don't know where God is leading us next. We are blessed to care for our four children. As a family, we're learning to care for our eight hens, blackberry bushes, blueberry trees, fig trees, grapes, a large vegetable garden, some herbs that aren't doing so well, and whoever God brings into our guest room. God has blessed our efforts abundantly. At every turn, needs have been met. Friends, family, and even strangers gave extra beds, furniture, dishes, and other items to supply our homestead with everything we need to help bring Christ's mercy to many. And who knows? Perhaps we will entertain angels.

Writing with St. Faustina

Catholics today have a great opportunity before us to speak to the world of Christ's unfathomable Divine Mercy. As a writer, I feel called to continue to spread the message of Divine Mercy throughout the world. Surely, St. Faustina has something to do with these efforts, as she was called to the same task.

So perhaps one of the most intimate ways in which St. Faustina impacts my spiritual life is through the example she set in sharing experiences in her *Diary*. What courage and faith it must have taken to record everything, not knowing what others would think! It has been said that when Gabriel appeared to Mary at the Annunciation, she immediately believed she was seeing an angel and doubted nothing. But St. Faustina experienced the effects of original sin and struggled immensely with doubt about her spiritual experiences, as all of us do. Yet she opens her heart to the world in the *Diary*, fearlessly sharing struggles, doubts, and even the intimate words Jesus spoke within her soul.

We all have capacity to open ourselves up to Christ as she did. What might Jesus speak into our lives if we give Him opportunity? What graces might be waiting for us on the other side of our daily Rosary? How many souls might be spared from hell with our dedication to recitation of the Chaplet of Divine Mercy? What new gardens might we be able to plant and nurture for Mary if we listen for His will?

Faustinum – The Association of the Apostles of Divine Mercy

Through prayer and with the intercession of St. Faustina, I continually felt called to pursue life in a third order. Particularly one centered on Divine Mercy, the Chaplet, and Our Lady of Mercy.

I found a wonderful international spiritual association called Faustinum, or the Association of Apostles of Divine Mercy, that is subordinate to the Archbishop of Krakow, Poland. It is connected with St. Faustina's order. While not technically a third order, Faustinum offers a few levels of participation. People all over the world can enroll first as a volunteer, then as a member, and then they may choose to participate in a four-year formation process that will lead them to become an Apostle of Divine Mercy. After this, personal vows are permitted at the hands of one's confessor. The whole association is set up to foster spiritual growth towards Christian perfection. Faustinum encourages people to come to know Jesus more intimately, to trust in Him, to proclaim the mystery of Divine Mercy to the whole world, and to implore mercy for the whole world.

I am thrilled to be a part of something so beautiful, and I am grateful that St. Faustina continues to lead me closer to her work and to the ocean of mercy.

Encountering Mercy

Saint Faustina recorded these words of spiritual counsel from Fr. Joseph Andrasz, SJ, in her *Diary*: "Act in a way that all those who come in contact with you will go away joyful. Sow happiness about you because you have received much from God; give, then, generously to others. They should take leave of you with their hearts filled with joy, even if they have no more than touched the hem of your garment" (*Diary*, 55).

God has blessed our family with abundance. To whom much is given, much is expected, and our family does not take this lightly. We do our best to share mercy with everyone we encounter, just as mercy has first been shown to us.

Whether we are serving a mother who opens the gift of a new outfit for her baby, a house guest who retires to clean, white linens, or a child who needs to borrow a dress because she didn't make it to the potty chair, hopefully those who experience even a small portion of the blessings God has given us to share will encounter the mercy of God.

Praise be to God our Merciful Father!
Jesus, we trust in You!

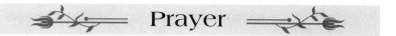

Prayer

Saint Faustina's prayer to Our Lady.

O Mary, Immaculate Virgin,
Pure crystal for my heart,
You are my strength, O secure anchor,
You are a shield and protection for a weak heart.

O Mary, you are pure and unparalleled,
Virgin and Mother at one and the same time;
You're beautiful as the sun, by nothing defiled.
Nothing is worthy of comparison to the image
of Your soul.

Your beauty enthralled the Thrice-Holy One's eye,
That He came down from heaven,
forsaking th'eternal See's throne,
And assumed from Your Heart Body and Blood,
Hiding for nine months in the Virgin's Heart.

O Mother, Virgin, this will no one comprehend,
That the infinite God is becoming a man;
It's only love's and His inscrutable mercy's purpose.
Through You, Mother — it's given us to live with
Him for ever.

O Mary, Virgin Mother and Heaven's Gate,
Through You salvation came to us;
Every grace to us streams forth through Your hands,
And faithful imitation of You only will sanctify me.

O Mother, Virgin — most beautiful Lily.
Your Heart was for Jesus the first tabernacle on earth,
And that, because Your humility was the deepest,

Wherefore You were raised above Angel choirs and Saints.

O Mary, my sweet Mother,
To You I turn over my soul, my body, and my poor heart.
Be the safeguard of my life,
Especially at death's hour, in the final fight.
(*Diary*, 161)

CHAPTER 7

Mercy Unseen

Lori Ubowski

"Eternal God, in whom mercy is endless and the treasury of compassion inexhaustible, look kindly upon us and increase Your mercy in us, that in difficult moments we might not despair nor become despondent, but with great confidence submit ourselves to Your holy will, which is Love and Mercy itself." (*Diary*, 950)

The stories of encounter I share are not tales of undying and inspiring devotion to Divine Mercy. They will not tell of years of tireless and dedicated prayer. If you asked me right now, I would not immediately or eloquently be able to quote the multitudes of beautiful words and revelations in the *Diary of Saint Maria Faustina Kowalska*. I wish that were the case! But what I can speak to is my appreciation for St. Faustina's example and the way that I can look to her in the same way I treasure a close friend who can relate to my struggles and journey with me through times of despair.

Saint Faustina constantly submitted herself to God's holy will in times of great despair and distress. She shares in her *Diary* regarding times of personal trial:

> After such sufferings the soul finds itself in a state of great purity of spirit and very close to God. But I should add that during these spiritual torments it is close to God, but it is blind. The soul's vision is

plunged into darkness, and though God is nearer than ever to the soul which is suffering, the whole secret consists in the fact that it knows nothing of this (*Diary*, 109).

I love her insight about how unaware we can be of God's Divine Mercy when we are in the thick of it with suffering and despair. She speaks of the blindness of suffering souls even as God is nearest to us in our times of suffering. I believe one of the greatest affirmations of Jesus' Divine Mercy is that His mercy is not withheld even from those who may struggle to see His gift.

My personal introduction to the Chaplet of Divine Mercy came in the form of song in early 2010. My husband Adam and I are both musicians and songwriters. A good friend of ours, also a musician and songwriter, reached out and asked if we would be interested in helping with a project of his. His devotion to Divine Mercy had inspired him to write music to accompany the Chaplet. He was in the process of gathering musicians to record vocals and instrumentals. Even though I had little personal exposure to the Chaplet at this point, I knew that I desired to be a part of this project, and I found it to be an incredibly moving experience.

I was humbled and honored to contribute to a labor of love that would serve to share the devotion of Divine Mercy with so many, and the Chaplet quickly became a beloved prayer for myself and my little ones. While my prayer life was sporadic at the time, and frankly still is, I would find myself singing along to the CD in the car with the kids as we drove around to different errands and activities. The Chaplet has become my go-to when I need comfort or reassurance during times of doubt, when I struggle to trust God, or when I simply do not have the time to pray an entire Rosary.

During this introduction to St. Faustina and Divine Mercy, Adam and I had no idea that we were about to face some significant struggles. What continues to amaze me about it all is that by entering into this sung prayer of the Chaplet together, we essentially were already asking for God's Divine Mercy for a situation of which we were not yet even aware. Still, we repeated those words at the end of the Chaplet, "Jesus, I trust in You." This declaration of trust would soon be tested.

Surrender=Trust

Adam and I met in college through the music department and a mutual friend. As cradle Catholics, we were both raised in an environment where music was an avenue for prayer and worship. We were both incredibly blessed to have people in our lives who mentored us, challenging us to grow in our musical skills as an expression of faith. In college, we shared this cultivated passion for music and worship through the avenue of campus ministry. Eventually, we got married and actually both settled into full-time music director positions, working in two neighboring parishes in northwest Florida. We were grateful for the opportunity to be employed in an area in which we were both knowledgeable and passionate, but which also gave us the opportunity to lead others to Christ through music.

By the 10th year of ministry, we experienced significant growth in our skills and spiritual maturity in our parishes as well as in our itinerant music ministry that took place outside the parish walls. We had also worked extensively on our songwriting. People responded to the music God had inspired our hearts to share, and we desired to reach more people with this inspiration. We worked and researched diligently to bring into reality these desires and aspirations we believed to be from God. We wanted to record these songs and record them well, offering our best. We found a producer and started calculating the kind of capital we needed to have in place, and also started identifying all of the many details involved in recording a full-length project. It was not a small price tag, and the list of tasks was long, but we forged ahead, trying to come up with some creative solutions for funding our project on parish salaries. In the midst of these exciting times, we came face to face with just how weak our trust in the Lord really was.

As we cared for our small — but growing — family and continued to pursue our passion for parish ministry, we worried about our future and how we would meet the growing financial demands placed upon our family. In Florida, especially in areas close in proximity to a beach or to a military base, the prospect of being a landlord is a fairly common opportunity. At the time, we thought we were being forward-thinking and smart about our future by keeping our house as a rental investment as we moved into a house that would provide a little more room for our growing family. In hindsight, what truly transpired was a misguided decision based on a lack of trust. We were musicians. What did we know about being landlords? The time and stress invested in worrying and in the maintenance of the rental property robbed us of peace and precious time with our family. This stress on our family was further compounded when we made the horrifying realization in between tenants that the house had been overrun by dreaded northwest Florida termites. In this small rectangular house, half of a short side and half of a long side were completely eaten inside the walls by termites, rendering it condemned, un-rentable, and unsellable. It was devastating. Even more heartbreaking was the realization that fixing the house so we could either rent it again or sell it (because we were definitely over the whole landlord thing) would take thousands of dollars.

Everything seemed to be falling to pieces. Our dreams were shattered, our financial future was uncertain, and we could see no feasible way out of this mess. Like St. Faustina as she faced opposition to her intense calling and desire to enter a convent, it was one of those situations that seems so dire you feel incapable of crying out, "Jesus, I trust in You!" The unspoken thought was, "Can even He fix this?"

Surrender. That is all we could do. Drawing strength from St. Faustina's example of abandoning herself completely to God's will, we tackled one thing at a time. First, it meant surrendering our lack of trust: We did not trust in God's providence for our future, and that led to some poor decisions. Then, it meant letting go of our dream: the great desire we had to record our music. That last step may have been the hardest because, since we believed this desire was truly from the Lord, when we began to doubt the foundation for these desires, it felt as if we were beginning to doubt the Lord. We had to search deep for answers to many questions. Were we perhaps making this dream all about us? It was about God, right? But if it was about God, how could it fail? Asking these questions and seeking their answers confirmed to us that we needed to be willing to surrender this desire completely and trust God's infinite wisdom and mercy. We reluctantly put the dream to bed and focused on how we were going to move forward. Giving up our dream was heartbreaking, and failing at our brief and fruitless capital venture was embarrassing. It was difficult to see beyond the struggles.

What happened in the following months helped us connect with the words Jesus spoke to St. Faustina: "**Do not be discouraged by the difficulties you encounter in proclaiming My mercy. These difficulties that affect you so painfully are needed for your sanctification and as evidence that this work is Mine**" (*Diary*, 1142). I was given so much comfort by these words. Our suffering is not in vain, and we can rest in the assurance that we will come out on the other end of these struggles made more whole, more complete, knowing the confidence of doing God's work, and fulfilling His plan and purpose.

Still struggling to find our footing and formulate our plan for "what's next?" we noticed one day that an unfamiliar company followed our music ministry profile on Twitter. Since we were by no means avid Twitter users, it is a small miracle that we even noticed, and we realized that the follower was a parishioner who had started a new business that specialized in refurbishing condemned houses in addition to working with legal counsel to help homeowners get out from under a condemned house. We could hardly believe it. This was just no coincidence. This was certainly God's mercy beginning to move in our lives. He sent the absolute right person at the absolute right time to help us out of an impossible situation. It sounds unbelievable, but they were able to fix everything and negotiate a way to lighten the financial burden of our troubled rental with only a few hundred dollars out of our pocket. The weight that was lifted is indescribable. It was a peace that undoubtedly came from the merciful Father. God was not done, though; He was just starting to show His power.

Adam and I continued our music ministry positions in two different parishes. This arrangement meant that we were unable to sing and play at the same Masses most of the time because of conflicting schedules, plus since we had young children at home at the time, we wanted one of us to be home with them whenever possible. On rare occasions, an opportunity would arise for Adam to join me to play guitar and sing for the Sunday evening Mass at the parish where I worked, since the parish where he worked did not have a late Sunday Mass. During one of these rare evenings, while we were still recovering from our rental house calamity, I looked out and noticed that in addition to the regular attendees, several people from Adam's work parish were in the Communion line. I attributed it to soccer tournaments and activities that would keep people from attending morning Masses. At the end of this Mass, we were halfway through our recessional song and I suddenly realized that no one was leaving. (You know what I'm talking about: the flood of regulars who bail the minute the priest starts walking down the aisle to leave.) My first logical thought was, "Oh, they must really like this song, or we are doing an okay job tonight." I could never have imagined what was about to happen next. The whole church stayed for the entire recessional song, and as we finished the final refrain, a few people approached the pulpit with the kind of comically giant check typically reserved for TV sweepstakes winners. They called us up and presented us with a financial gift that had been raised secretly by people from both of our parishes in order to fund our first recording! Words could not express my overwhelming gratitude. I sobbed ... for two weeks.

What an absolute gift and outpouring of God's mercy! The generosity was not only in the realization of our surrendered dreams and desires but, more overwhelmingly, in what was essentially their commissioning of us and our ministry. This incredible gift — that we did not earn or deserve — was not meant for us to go forth just as Adam and Lori to share this music, but rather, it was meant for us to go forth as an extension, a representation of every single person who was a part of making the project a reality. It was greater confirmation that calmed the doubts we had about being able to use this project to glorify God rather than ourselves, since we were, in a sense, taken out of the equation. We did not make this happen. God's faithful sons and daughters combined efforts so that all of us together could work to further His glory and His Gospel, fulfilling Jesus' promise, **"When a soul approaches me with trust, I fill it with such an abundance of graces that it cannot contain them within itself, but radiates them to other souls"** (*Diary*, 1074).

Even though this whole experience began with desolation and despair, it was a process of God sanctifying us and doing His work in us. Had we not faced trials of faith and trust, we would not have been able to appreciate fully the divine mission and the responsibility that had been given to us. I continue to see God's limitless mercy at work in other areas of our lives, as well: My mission does not end with this one experience or story. God continues to remind me that His graces are abundant, and that I am called to share these graces with others.

Continued Grace

Jesus told St. Faustina, **"You are a sweet grape in a chosen cluster; I want others to have a share in the juice that is flowing within you"** (*Diary*, 393).

A few years ago, one of my best friends, who had been my college roommate and a bridesmaid of mine, sent me a copy of *Divine Mercy for Moms* by Michele Faehnle and Emily Jaminet for Mother's Day. This book was a sweet and thoughtful gift, perfect for my season of life at the time. (My youngest was old enough that I could actually hope to finish a book again!) I appreciated this gift so much because it allowed me to share in experiencing something that had impacted her life, plus I was equally blessed to spend time with reflections that spoke to my life as a mom of three, navigating the waters of work, ministry, and trying my best to raise pleasant and faithful little human beings. At this time, I was also feeling moved by the Holy Spirit to expand my musical talents for the Lord and go deeper into working with women's ministry. I asked my friend Erin, who was from the same town as Michele and Emily, and knew them from church, to connect us. Little did I know, my friend St. Faustina was tapping me on the shoulder and moving pieces that I could have never arranged myself.

When I had the opportunity a year later to help re-record an updated version of the Chaplet of Divine Mercy with some amazing musicians, I was again struck by the power of singing this prayer. Embracing the beauty and emotion brought forth by the words and the music moved me just like it had before. Reminiscing about how it felt to record it the first time around, all those years ago, created a sense of reflection and appreciation for how far I had come in faith and trust, as well as the effect these lessons had on future prayers and choices.

As a result of being a part of this new project, I unexpectedly found myself at the Catholic Marketing Network conference in Chicago. This second recording had led me more intimately into a friendship with St. Faustina, and I came to understand more fully her mission to spread the devotion to Divine Mercy to the entire world, even after her death. This task given to her by Jesus seems like it would have been so impossible for a young, uneducated woman living in a convent, and yet here I was, decades later and half a world away, not only benefiting from the devotion to Divine Mercy, but joining the mission to spread it, too. As I sat in the display booth in front of a large Divine Mercy Image, a replica of the exact image that was painted under the direction of St. Faustina from her mystical visions of Jesus in 1934, Michele Faehnle came up to me and introduced herself, explaining she was there promoting her book, *Divine Mercy for Moms*.

My jaw hit the floor as I realized this "God-incidence" unfolding before my eyes. I told Michele who I was, and how we were supposed to meet in just a few weeks in Columbus, Ohio. She was equally as surprised and delighted, and invited me to lunch. God's Divine Mercy once again began to overwhelm me in so many ways.

Sometimes you know God is moving in your life when you get to the point of saying, "You just can't make this stuff up!" Even though Michele, Emily, and I were all at the same conference without knowing it and thus met each other a few weeks early, it is clear that God definitely had bigger plans than just introducing us. My intent to connect with them had been prompted by my desire to be more involved in an apostolate of service to women, and my hope was that they could help me with discernment in this area. Our unexpected early introduction, not a coincidence but by design, began an instant friendship and catapulted my desires into reality. God wanted me to begin to grow in this new apostolate, and He meant NOW! Not only was I affirmed in this desire, but I left that faith-filled meeting with an introduction to an editor who has encouraged me to pursue sharing the words and the mission on my heart for the bond between mothers and daughters journeying together by publishing *Side by Side: A Catholic Mother-Daughter Journal* (Ave Maria Press, 2018).

As I reflect upon how intensely God's mercy continues to move in my life in these and in so many other circumstances, I marvel at the unfathomable abundance of graces He generously pours out on me as I continue to seek and to follow Him. Jesus said to St. Faustina, **"My child you are My delight, you are the comfort of My Heart. I grant you as many graces as you can hold. As often as you want to make Me happy, speak to the world about My great and unfathomable mercy"** (*Diary*, 164). These words resonate so well with me as I appreciate the trials, the struggles, and the sanctification by fire that have prepared me to realize and accept the graces that God has poured out on me so that I may share them with others through music, through words, through friendships, through love, through trust, and through the spreading of the message of Divine Mercy.

Saint Faustina, pray for us.

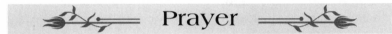

Prayer

The Chaplet of Divine Mercy

How to Recite the Chaplet

The Chaplet of Mercy is recited using ordinary Rosary beads of five decades. The Chaplet is preceded by two opening prayers from the *Diary* of St. Faustina and followed by a closing prayer.

1. Make the Sign of the Cross

In the name of the Father, and of the Son, and of the Holy Spirit. Amen.

2. Optional Opening Prayers

You expired, Jesus, but the source of life gushed forth for souls, and the ocean of mercy opened up for the whole world. O Fount of Life, unfathomable Divine Mercy, envelop the whole world and empty Yourself out upon us.

(Repeat three times)

O Blood and Water, which gushed forth from the Heart of Jesus as a fount of Mercy for us, I trust in You!

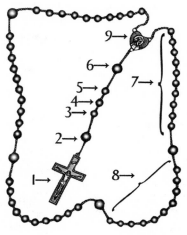

3. Our Father

Our Father, Who art in heaven, hallowed be Thy name; Thy kingdom come; Thy will be done on earth as it is in heaven. Give us this day our daily bread; and forgive us our trespasses as we forgive those who trespass against us; and lead us not into temptation, but deliver us from evil, Amen.

4. Hail Mary

Hail Mary, full of grace. The Lord is with thee. Blessed art thou amongst women, and blessed is the fruit of thy womb, Jesus. Holy Mary, Mother of God, pray for us sinners, now and at the hour of our death, Amen.

5. The Apostles' Creed

I believe in God, the Father almighty, Creator of heaven and earth, and in Jesus Christ, His only Son, our Lord, who was conceived by the Holy Spirit, born of the Virgin Mary, suffered under Pontius Pilate, was crucified, died and was buried; He descended into hell; on the third day He rose again from the dead; He ascended into heaven, and is seated at the right hand of God the Father almighty; from there He will come to judge the living and the dead. I believe in the Holy Spirit, the holy catholic Church, the communion of saints, the forgiveness of sins, the resurrection of the body, and life everlasting. Amen.

6. The Eternal Father *(on the Our Father beads)*

Eternal Father, I offer you the Body and Blood, Soul and Divinity of Your Dearly Beloved Son, Our Lord, Jesus Christ, in atonement for our sins and those of the whole world.

7. On the 10 Small Beads of Each Decade

For the sake of His sorrowful Passion, have mercy on us and on the whole world.

8. Repeat for the remaining decades

Saying the "Eternal Father" on the "Our Father" bead and then 10 "For the sake of His sorrowful Passion" on the following "Hail Mary" beads.

9. Conclude with Holy God *(Repeat three times)*

Holy God, Holy Mighty One, Holy Immortal One, have mercy on us and on the whole world.

10. Optional Closing Prayer

Eternal God, in whom mercy is endless and the treasury of compassion inexhaustible, look kindly upon us and increase Your mercy in us, that in difficult moments we might not despair nor become despondent, but with great confidence submit ourselves to Your holy will, which is Love and Mercy itself.

CHAPTER 8

Language of the Soul

Chiara Finaldi

"Jesus have mercy on me; do not entrust such great things to me, as You see that I am a bit of dust and completely inept." (*Diary*, 53)

Throughout my life, the Image of the Divine Mercy had always been in the background. In my hometown of Palermo, Italy, many churches displayed a reproduction of Jesus with the pale and red rays flowing from His chest. The image of the risen Christ that St. Faustina received in the 1930s was a common sight in many of the shops and homes of my neighborhood. The two bakeries my family owned had a replica hanging above the register, and my grandparents kept a faded copy on their dresser. As for me, every time I was given one, I would quickly get rid of it by bringing it to one of my old relatives or neighbors. I thought it was an image that represented a dated devotion, stuck in the past and destined to stay there, an image for grandparents and for those lacking in artistic taste. Little did I know ... .

Many years later in 2016, after a moment of discouragement, as work, the lack of space in the house, and the workload of the family seemed to be crushing me, this image reappeared in my life. During that difficult time, I felt called to visit a local Catholic bookshop that had a chapel in the back where the Blessed Sacrament was exposed most days. I had moved to England in 1999 after marrying my sweetheart at the age of 19, but even though I had lived in Southeast London since my arrival, this was the first time I had entered that place. The Lord knew how much I needed Him at that particular moment of my life, and He wanted to be found.

I started going to the chapel daily. The Divine Mercy Image was right there by the tabernacle, once again accompanying me silently. To my surprise, the attraction towards that image of Jesus grew stronger. I wanted to know more about it; I wanted to understand why this painting, in modern terms, had "gone viral."

When I got home, the first thing I did was to go online to find out who the artist was behind this Jesus of Mercy, when it all happened, how, and why? No matter what search terms I entered, a certain saint named Faustina and her *Diary* kept coming up. The natural consequence to all this research was to buy the book, wherein I would hopefully find the answers to all my questions. Meanwhile, while surfing on one of my Facebook groups, I found out that someone named Michele Faehnle was looking for people to review a new book on Divine Mercy that was tailored to mothers. I rarely put my name forward for this kind of thing, since as a mother of six with a large extended family around, I can hardly ever commit to anything, let alone to reading a whole book. But it was different this time: I was determined to get through at least this thin book.

At first I was underwhelmed. The 95-page book looked too simple, but I dove in anyway. Without realizing it, it opened the door to St. Faustina and the Divine Mercy devotion. The introduction to the book cites a quotation from St. John Paul II upon his arrival at Fatima on May 12, 1982, shortly before the anniversary of the attempt on his life: "In the designs of Providence, there are no mere coincidences!" I knew then that it was not by chance that my path crossed Michele's. Because of this little book, I plucked up the courage to open my mind to St. Faustina's wisdom and childlike faith. Also, by applying it to the life of a mother, I was able to unlock my heart and change my narrow-minded attitude towards a time-tested devotion.

Do It for Me

After reading *Divine Mercy for Moms*, I dove straight into St Faustina's *Diary*. How could I have been so foolish as to allow myself to be deceived by snobbery about the image? What consoled me was that even St. Faustina felt a bit uneasy with that picture: "Who will paint You as beautiful as You are?" (*Diary*, 313) As my journey to explore what was meant by "Divine Mercy" progressed through Faustina's writing, that picture became more and more meaningful. "**Not in the beauty of the color, nor of the brush lies the greatness of this image, but in My grace**" (*Diary*, 313), Jesus said to the little saint, and that stayed with me.

The more I read about Faustina, the more I wanted to know about her and her total surrender to Christ. Her simplicity touched me deeply. Her meekness and her immense strength and trust in the Lord were astonishing. My understanding of what it means to serve God was shaken.

I got married when I was 19 and became a mother a year later, just a few weeks after turning 20. With a new baby, I did not have time to attend college. On top of it all, I moved to England and had to learn a new language. In this new life, I always felt inadequate whenever anyone asked me to do a job. Many times I wished I were like those wonderful apologists: eloquent, knowledgeable, and courageous. I was at times upset with God that I had not been given the same gifts to study the faith diligently and boldly defend it. The temptation to think that I was not going to be much use to God because of my limitations was always present. I had an ideal in my mind of how I was supposed to serve God that did not seem to match His. Fortunately, I found many answers to dispel these temptations and doubts in the *Diary*.

As I read about the life of this young girl originally named Helen Kowalska, I found the ordinary life of an ordinary girl, who had nothing by the world's standards. This was a girl with a very common surname and a poor background, a girl who could hardly read and write in her own language. The more

I looked for greatness in her, the more I discovered poverty, weakness, and humanity.

In the *Diary*, I read about this young sister who completed humble tasks with the other sisters of lower education and social status. I found stories of daily routines and ordinary relationships, and I followed her life from the kitchen to the chapel, from the garden to the confessional, waiting to see God act.

At first, the way she wrote was too simple for my tastes, and her relationship with Jesus was almost too sweet and surreal to believe. I started my friendship with Faustina perhaps like many of the sisters in the convent did, doubting her visions, but then something changed: The more I read, the more I wanted to read. The more Faustina's soul spoke to my soul, the more I wanted to know about the beautiful love story between her and her Beloved. I could not wait to hear what Jesus had to say, and for some time I could not go to bed without having read at least a couple of entries from the *Diary*.

In the following months, Faustina became part of my family. Not a day would pass without my retelling a story or a passage from the *Diary* to my children. I often mentioned to my mother's group in the parish that this outpouring of the mercy of our Lord is available, if we are willing to accept it.

Faustina's struggles were human and real. In them, I could identify some of my very own struggles in my daily tasks as a woman and in my vocation as a wife and mother. Her misunderstandings with some of the sisters, the lack of strength when undertaking some chores, and her idea of service were all very relatable. However, her response to even the littlest suffering was a long way away from mine: Everything — and I mean everything — she did was done for the glory of God and not for herself. In humiliation, she found joy, and in offering up all of her sufferings, she was closer to Christ than ever before.

Why could I not be more like St. Faustina? Why was I rarely able to rest in the Lord in my struggles? Why would I quickly turn suffering into moaning and complaining? I will tell you why! Because I often dismissed my ordinary life and the possibility that God can act in me in a way that would speak of Him to the world. How can one serve the Lord among piles of laundry, dirty pots, school runs, and coffee mornings? I found that unlike Faustina, though my lips said many times, "Jesus, I trust in You," my heart did not really mean it.

It was within the walls of a convent that Faustina had her encounter with Christ. There, her relationship with Jesus flourished and raised her to holiness. She found Him in every action of the day; she saw Him in every person she met. God called her to serve Him there, then He showed her the way. Above all, she allowed Him to abide in her — therein lay her strength:

> Once, when I returned to my cell, I was so tired that I had to rest a moment before I started to undress, and when I was already undressed, one of the sisters asked me to fetch her some hot water. Although I was tired, I dressed quickly and brought her the water she wanted, even though it was quite a long walk from the cell to the kitchen, and the mud was ankle-deep. When I re-entered my cell, I saw the ciborium with the Blessed Sacrament, and I heard this voice, **Take this ciborium and bring it to the tabernacle**. I hesitated at first, but when I approached and touched it, I heard these words, **Approach each of the sisters with the same love with which you approach Me; and whatever you do for them, you do it for Me**. A moment later, I saw that I was alone (*Diary*, 285).

I had been so busy looking for the perfect way to serve the Lord that I missed countless opportunities to serve Him. He wanted me to treat every action of my daily routine as another way to praise Him, rather than how I had been treating them — as a military campaign to be survived.

It was a sudden realization that Christ was very close to me, too. Even though I hadn't paid attention to Him, what with the busyness of a mother's life, He was still there, ready for me to love Him by giving my whole self with no reservations, without holding anything back. As Jesus told Faustina, **"My love deceives no one"** (*Diary*, 29).

Christ wanted me to serve Him through my children: to clothe Him, accompany Him, feed Him, and give Him water through them. He wanted me to do all this with a humble heart, on a daily basis. I am sure most mothers would agree when I say that it is not as easy as it sounds, especially when clean clothes, food, and drink seem to be required at the most inopportune moments. On this journey to holiness, I do not always remember that Christ is also in my children, my husband, and my neighbor, but when I do, I find such joy in serving them.

His Words are My Words

Being cradle Catholics, we can become so familiar with the faith that we take for granted many aspects of the Liturgy and Sacraments. Thanks to St. Faustina, my relationship with Christ was pushed towards something deeper, and my relationship with the Sacrament of Reconciliation was revived. Throughout her religious life, St. Faustina was asked to go to the confessional very regularly. Meeting with her confessor was an important part of her spiritual growth. Jesus told St. Faustina, **"When you approach the confessional, know this, that I Myself am waiting there for you. I am only hidden by the priest, but I Myself act in your soul"** (*Diary*, 1602). He encouraged her to **"tell him everything and reveal your soul to him ... . Do not fear anything"** (*Diary*, 232). I read these lines from the *Diary* as if I were discovering something new, even though I grew up always knowing that the priest was acting *in persona Christi* in the Sacraments and, as such, was able to administer special sanctifying graces. In the confessional, the priest truly had the God-given authority to absolve my sins.

I tried to go as often as I could to Reconciliation, but realized that what I had considered "often" was not enough.

If Faustina — a saint — had so much to confess in such a short time, how could I struggle to find sins to confess from one month to the next? I must be getting it all wrong.

Thanks to my friend Faustina, my approach to Confession changed from a mechanical habit into a genuine need to deepen a relationship. I could show who I really was, without fear or shame, and desire to hear Jesus' voice and advice. Every time I walk towards the confessional now, my heart is filled with joy because I have the certain hope that I will meet Christ's mercy and immense love for me. Even if sometimes I meet a half-hearted or tired priest, I know that the grace will be poured upon me all the same.

A Message of Love from Jesus

When my husband, Pierpaolo, and I first started dating, I lived in Sicily and he was in London with no Internet, Skype, or social media. We spent three years of our courtship writing a letter a day. Although reading about our feelings and desires for the future was wonderful, the need for physical contact was overwhelming. I wanted to hold his hand, to see him face to face, and to hear his voice in person. To spend time together was vital if our relationship was going to advance.

I began to feel the same way about my relationship with Jesus. Christ waited patiently for me in the same little chapel every Thursday afternoon. When for one reason or another I couldn't go for a number of weeks, I started experiencing that same feeling I experienced when dating Pierpaolo. That desire to see Him, to be around Him, filled my soul. His Real Presence felt more real and finally became not just a concept but also something I could physically experience. Thanks to St. Faustina's words of strength and truth, I rediscovered the freshness and the beauty of a relationship that had become stale because of me.

Before the Blessed Sacrament, I had the most beautiful declaration of love from Christ! Moved by St. Faustina's experience, I had the courage to allow Jesus to speak to me in a language that is not English or Italian. This was a language that doesn't need words but clearly speaks to the soul. This was a language that encourages, above all, accepting Him as Lord of my life, with all my defects and imperfections. Reading about St. Faustina's frequent visits to her Beloved in the tabernacle was such a beautiful reminder that if I wanted my relationship with Jesus to grow and to flourish, I needed to spend time with Him alone. In this moment of intimacy, I needed to silently listen in order to get to know Him better.

The more I visited the chapel, the more the voice of the Beloved was clear. It didn't matter that my English wasn't perfect, it didn't matter that I was terrified of talking in front of people. It didn't matter that I didn't have a degree or that I wasn't a great apologist for the faith. My family and I had received so much that I could not keep the gift for myself. I felt pushed; I felt an incredible urge to reach out to other women to tell them about this Merciful Love that turns lives upside down, and always for the better.

Sharing the Merciful Love

I was already running a Facebook group called "Catholic Mothers" and occasionally writing for our family blog as well as other Catholic blogs. But God wanted something more from me! The idea of a Catholic mothers' conference was pressing me and would not abandon me. The Catholic population in the UK is a minority, so I knew a conference in England would be tiny in comparison to conferences in the United States, but something within me kept insisting I had to try. I was in touch with Michele Faehnle, and her encouragement was decisive. She even set a date for me: The conference would take place on Divine Mercy weekend. I unceasingly called upon St Faustina's intercession for the success of the event. The program was very clear in my head: I wanted women to come back from this weekend regenerated in their vocation as women, wives, and mothers, and above all as beloved daughters of God. I wanted for them to experience His loving Mercy, to go home ready to serve their family and fulfil their own calling to sainthood.

Could I really achieve so much? A woman from Palermo, Sicily, whose English was not perfect, with no titles or qualifications? A woman who has been a mother most of her life and has very little experience of the world? No! I couldn't do it! But God could.

In Faustina's notes, I met a girl who had no fear of being led by God, a girl who was at God's complete disposal, because she knew Christ was her strength. Her limitations were not too much of a concern or an obstacle because she trusted in Him. In the same manner, I was being invited to trust in Him, too. The Divine Mercy Image accompanied me throughout the preparation for the conference. Every day I drew strength from this picture and relied on the trust that Faustina had put in Jesus her whole life. Organizing the conference was tiring, but it was never difficult. Every step was already laid out and prepared ahead of time for me. God obviously wanted this to happen! The only other event I can recall in my life panning out so smoothly was when Pierpaolo and I decided to get married a year before we had planned. It took only four months to organize our entire wedding. For us, that has always been a sign of God's blessing. The same thing happened during the organization of this conference, and I had never been so sure in my life that He was there before me leading the way.

On Divine Mercy Weekend, 125 participants from all over England and beyond gathered at the Carmelite Priory of Aylesford in the UK, where St. Simon Stock received the Brown Scapular from Our Lady. This was an occasion for these women to rest in the Lord and build new faith-filled friendships. Our Lady of Mount Carmel seemed ready to shower the women who attended, and those who followed the conference online, with many graces. In addition to great talks and workshops, there was also the opportunity to have a moment of intimacy with the Lord in the Blessed Sacrament — something many mothers, especially those with young children, rarely had. Faustina taught me how vital spending time with the Real Presence was, and I wanted to share that lesson with the women there.

For the first time in Britain, the conference had the honor of hosting Gianna Emanuela Molla, the daughter for whom St. Gianna Beretta Molla gave up her life. I miraculously managed to contact her through the combined efforts of St. Gianna and St. Faustina. She was a walking, talking reminder of a very modern saint, bearing witness to her mother's love, a love that God willed would reach the whole world. Not only was it the first time Gianna Emanuela had come to England to spread devotion to her mother, but it was also the first time she found herself talking about her mother before an audience exclusively made up of mothers. The sanctity of life was praised, and so was motherhood, which is the way to holiness for many women.

Laughter and tears filled the room and a deeper communion with the saints was established. As I was (and still am) on this journey of discovering Divine Mercy, I asked a Polish priest of the Marian Fathers of the Immaculate Conception (MIC) — who are particularly devoted to promoting the Divine Mercy — to speak about St. Faustina, the Divine Mercy devotion, and Our Lady, the ultimate Catholic mother and Mother of the Divine Mercy. His words made the love of God for humanity echo within us. As he held up the life-size image of the Divine Mercy, which he had brought with him for the occasion, he invited us all to look up. That very same gaze that Jesus offered to mankind on Golgotha greeted us. The picture, the priest explained, was meant to capture the same merciful eyes that once looked down from the Cross. The overflowing rays from His side spoke of the abundant mercy available to us through the Sacraments. His breaking out of the darkness of the background announced Jesus' victory over death and sin. Jesus' feet striding towards us meant that He will surely come to us if we are open to receiving Him. That picture I once despised became something I wanted to behold forever!

"Are you ready for Him to step forward towards you?" Father asked. "His love doesn't deceive anyone! Can you see His outpouring of mercy in this picture? His love for you and me? If you can, then with confidence say, 'Jesus, I trust in You'; because if you do, you will not regret it!"

As we finished praying the Chaplet together, Father took out from his suitcase a first class relic of St. Faustina and placed it on the main table for us to venerate. I had no doubt that she had been interceding for me, and when I knelt down before the reliquary, her words resounded within me: "I feel certain that my mission will not come to an end upon my death, but will begin. O doubting souls, I will draw aside for you the veils of heaven to convince you of God's goodness, so that you will no longer continue to wound with your distrust the sweetest Heart of Jesus. God is Love and Mercy" (*Diary*, 281).

When I stood up and turned around, a long line of women waited to venerate this wonderful saint. I could no longer see myself, my limitations, my weaknesses, or my fears. The gaze from the Cross was upon me. I could see His immense mercy for me and had the certainty that He could do marvelous things even with a speck of dust like me. He could do the impossible, if only I denied myself, recognized my limitations with humility, and accepted His infinite Mercy with no reservation.

I needed to welcome Him in my life and truly declare with all my heart:

JESUS, I TRUST IN YOU!

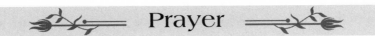

Prayer

Saint Faustina's considerations on Divine Mercy to help a soul become trusting.

Divine Mercy, gushing forth from the bosom of the Father, I trust in You.

Divine Mercy, greatest attribute of God, I trust in You

Divine Mercy, incomprehensible mystery, I trust in You.

Divine Mercy, fount gushing forth from the mystery of the Most Blessed Trinity, I trust in You.

Divine Mercy, unfathomed by any intellect, human or angelic, I trust in You.

Divine Mercy, from which wells forth all life and happiness, I trust in You.

Divine Mercy, better than the heavens, I trust in You.

Divine Mercy, source of miracles and wonders, I trust in You.

Divine Mercy, encompassing the whole universe, I trust in You.

Divine Mercy, descending to earth in the Person of the Incarnate Word, I trust in You.

Divine Mercy, which flowed out from the open wound of the Heart of Jesus, I trust in You.

Divine Mercy, enclosed in the Heart of Jesus for us, and especially for sinners, I trust in You.

Divine Mercy, unfathomed in the institution of the Sacred Host, I trust in You.

Divine Mercy, in the founding of Holy Church,
I trust in You.

Divine Mercy, in the Sacrament of Holy Baptism,
I trust in You.

Divine Mercy, in our justification through Jesus Christ,
I trust in You.

Divine Mercy, accompanying us through our whole life,
I trust in You.

Divine Mercy, embracing us especially at the hour of
death, I trust in You.

Divine Mercy, endowing us with immortal life,
I trust in You.

Divine Mercy, accompanying us every moment of our
life, I trust in You.

Divine Mercy, shielding us from the fire of hell,
I trust in You.

Divine Mercy in the conversion of hardened sinners,
I trust in You.

Divine Mercy astonishment for Angels,
incomprehensible to Saints, I trust in You.

Divine Mercy, unfathomed in all the mysteries of God,
I trust in You.

Divine Mercy, lifting us out of every misery,
I trust in You.

Divine Mercy, source of our happiness and joy,
I trust in You.

Divine Mercy, in calling us forth from nothingness to
existence, I trust in You.

Divine Mercy, embracing all the works of His hands,
I trust in You.

Divine Mercy, crown of all of God's handiwork,
    I trust in You.

Divine Mercy, in which we are all immersed,
    I trust in You.

Divine Mercy, sweet relief for anguished hearts,
    I trust in You.

Divine Mercy, only hope of despairing souls,
    I trust in You.

Divine Mercy, repose of hearts, peace amidst fear,
    I trust in You.

Divine Mercy, delight and ecstasy of holy souls,
    I trust in You.

Divine Mercy, inspiring hope against all hope,
    I trust in You.

Eternal God, in whom mercy is endless and the treasury of compassion inexhaustible, look kindly upon us and increase Your mercy in us, that in difficult moments we might not despair nor become despondent, but with great confidence submit ourselves to Your holy will, which is Love and Mercy itself. (*Diary*, 949-950)

CHAPTER 9

Talk to Me, Friend to Friend: St. Faustina's Cure for Loneliness

Lis Luwia

Through this story I'm going to share, I would like to introduce my friend Faustina as I know her today. Although we have not been friends for very long, she has turned my idea of friendship upside down and has pushed me into a beautiful, budding friendship with our Lord, Jesus Christ. I hope that those who read this story will let her work wonders in their lives and gently push them closer to Christ, who encompasses everything good one could want in a best friend.

I do not think anyone wants to admit it even to themselves, least of all to other people, but sometimes life gets lonely. Stay-at-home parents are especially vulnerable to feeling pulled into loneliness as hours pass by without speaking to anyone over the age of 4. And if those parents are staying home with a baby who cannot speak yet, they can go downright crazy.

Recently married and learning the ropes as a new mom, I began to feel the vast emptiness of my house as the hours ticked by while my husband was at school and my newborn (who could not even smile yet) seesawed between eating and sleeping. I enjoyed those sweet baby cuddles, but I really did not know what to do with myself in all that silence. (What I would not give for a weekend of that now!) I began to feel the pull of loneliness in my soul. Had I truly known then that "the pull" was Jesus calling me, I might have gotten more involved in my parish, had a greater focus on my spiritual life, joined a

Bible study, and learned how to pray the Rosary. I might have allowed Him to consume me instead of tiptoeing the perimeter as I did. However, God works in His own perfect time, and like so many other people, my eyes had to be opened in a special way in order to be able to see clearly.

As a result of this feeling of loneliness, I was glad to go back to work when my daughter was three months old. Even though I was happy to be working again, I cried daily when I left my sweet baby in the morning. My husband was in school and was able to stay at home with her on most days. Deep, deep down, in that shut-tight part of my heart, I wanted to be the one at home with her. But I did not have a choice at this point because someone had to work, and my husband had to be in school. I pushed my yearnings aside and carried on. I kept myself busy so I wouldn't feel the loneliness. I focused on my job and told myself that I could not manage being alone with a babbling baby in an otherwise empty house any longer. The loneliness (and mom-guilt derived from feeling that way) that was creeping in was too much for me, so I was glad (at least, that is what I told myself) to put my maternity leave behind me.

Fast forward several years and another child later. My husband was accepted into medical school several states away, so I left my job as we moved our family of four and all of our belongings across the country to start on this new adventure. It was my first time staying at home with my two girls, aside from maternity leaves and short vacations. I felt like I had to learn how to mother all over again. I also felt like I was in way over my head, at a loss for how to manage even grocery shopping with extra (uncontrollable) bodies, and the loneliness I had felt before came flooding back.

We were in a new city, far from any family, friends, or any support network. On top of all of that, my husband had fallen off of our family's grid because of school; studying became more natural to him than sleeping; and even when he was home, his nose was in a book. Long gone were our lively chats over dinner and cuddles on the couch talking about our days.

The lines under his eyes spoke volumes, and his mind was constantly someplace else. We had to arrange stay-at-home date nights around his test schedules, and sometimes we would go days without a real conversation.

But medical school inherently comes with these sorts of challenges, and my expectations for this time period were fairly realistic. I knew going in that I would not get a lot of time with him. Medical school demanded retention of the knowledge acquired over the course of four years, which requires a lot of time, effort, and brainpower. So I gave my husband space and loved on him as best I could, but I needed a listening ear. I needed a friend.

I could talk to my friends from back home on the phone, but I knew I had to find a friend in this new city and time zone. I needed someone to sit beside me as I shared my heart, and especially, someone over the age of 4 with whom I could have a real conversation and feel like an adult again. Making new friends can be a hard thing to do, and I have always found it especially difficult. I had not had to go out of my way to make friends since my long-gone college days. And even then, I had a great assigned roommate and so I did not have to look very far to find a friend; that friendship had been practically handed to me. So I decided to start my new search for friendship in a safe space, a place where I could dip my toes without having to take the plunge immediately: I started a blog.

As I delved into the blogosphere, I discovered many wonderful, positive Catholic women. Their writings inspired me and pushed me to become a better Catholic mother, and I found a way to have quality communication with other adults. We had a Catholic Facebook group, and other Catholic women were even contributing to my blog; both great ways to be in touch with other adults during the day. I soon became online buddies with women from Florida, the Midwest, Colorado, and California. They were everywhere and so incredibly friendly, but the loneliness did not go away. It was still there. The blog and online friends were wonderful, but they were not enough.

I worked up the courage and took the next steps toward in-person friends. I joined the moms' group at church and started taking my girls to Storytime at the library, two things I had never gotten to do while working. Since I was new to being a stay-at-home mom, I felt like an odd black sheep. I was nervous in social circles and I was desperate for a friend. To make matters worse, I knew these relationships would be short-lived since my husband would have to move for medical rotations in two years. The other moms seemed so content with their lives, and I was still trying to figure it all out.

My husband tried to encourage me. "You can do it," he would urge. "Just ask someone for their number and make a playdate." It became something of a game for me. I would ask random people for their phone numbers just to try to build my confidence and take a shot at making a friend. I got a number from a mom at the playground, another number from a mom at the library, and a number from a mom in the checkout line at the grocery store (plus an odd look from the cashier). In hindsight, I could have tried to be less awkward, but I was doing my best at the time. I followed up, made playdates, and met some truly amazing women. They even taught this California girl how to stay sane during the long winter months and where to buy winter gear second hand.

As I grew in my confidence as a stay-at-home mom and learned how to juggle two kids while running errands, I realized that something was still missing: I still felt the void. My wonderful children could not fill the void, blogging could not fill the void, online friendships had not filled the void, and now these fantastic friendships I was building could not fill the void.

Part of the problem, of course, was that I missed my husband. That dear man was working so hard in school and did not have time for much else. When he did have time, I would ask him to spend time with the kids to fulfill their much-needed Daddy time. But even missing him did not account for the depth of the void I felt. It was a different kind of yearning that I could not quite put my finger on, something that even a really great girls' night out did not seem to fix.

During Confession one day, the priest mentioned a book, *Diary of Saint Maria Faustina Kowalska: Divine Mercy in My Soul.* "Have you read it?" he asked. I had heard of it once before, and it sounded interesting, so I had purchased it, but since then, the book had been sitting unread on my bookshelf, quietly gathering dust. He urged me to give it a try. Since his words were not the first sign I had gotten that I should actually read it instead of letting it become a dusty decoration, I cracked it open.

It was easy to fall in love with St. Faustina and her sweet, simple nature. I started out reading pages upon pages every night until one day it struck me that, at some point, I would finish the book, and it would make me so sad to see it end. I did not stop reading her *Diary* completely, but I began limiting myself to a few entries from the book every day, taking time to reflect on what I had read. I would carry her words with me through the day and think about them, think about St. Faustina, and think about my children and amazing spouse. I let her speak to my heart. Slowly, she transformed me, and I found a new friend. In fact, my first saint friend: St. Faustina.

In all the time I had spent praying that God would help me find a friend, I did not specify her height or how many kids she would have; I did not ask God for a friend who could babysit my kids or bake me a casserole when I gave birth again. The things I needed in a friend were not things I could check off of a list; it was soul-stirring conversations and companionship, a sister in Christ upon whom I could rely. And God knew exactly what I needed.

But God did not stop by giving me what I needed. Psalm 37:4 says, "Find your delight in the Lord, who will give you your heart's desire." Without knowing what it was I was longing for in a friendship (or maybe not knowing how beautiful a friendship God had planned for me), Jesus provided it to me. You see, Faustina also felt the same loneliness that I did:

Jesus, Friend of a lonely heart, You are my haven, You are my peace. You are my salvation, You are my serenity in moments of struggle and amidst an ocean of doubts. You are the bright ray that lights up the path of my life. You are everything to a lonely soul. You understand the soul even though it remains silent. You know our weaknesses and, like a good physician, You comfort and heal, sparing us sufferings — expert that You are (*Diary*, 247).

My friend, Faustina, led me closer to Jesus, to that haven and peace that He is. Through her *Diary*, St. Faustina opened my eyes to an innocent trust in Christ, and through her prayers she has helped to form me into a better wife, mother, and disciple of Christ. Through my bond with Faustina, my eyes were opened to the opportunities that awaited me in spiritual friendships. I asked Jesus to lead me to more saint friends. I would read about their lives, celebrate their feast days, and pray to them during the day. They became my own little posse, my support system and confidants. But I still wanted more. I asked my friend Faustina what I should do. Like a good friend who knows exactly what to do, she led me right to the Source and I slowly began to befriend Jesus.

Many years earlier, I attended an evangelical Christian university, and attending chapel service was required three times per week. I was quickly introduced to a plethora of worship songs and amazing speakers. I enjoyed the music and speakers, but one of the worship songs in particular made me uncomfortable as we sang, "Jesus is a friend of mine." I found myself listening to the song, but not singing it or even believing it. I had always understood Jesus as Savior and King of all, but I couldn't imagine that someone like Him would want to be friends with someone like me. I was sure these Protestant friends of mine had gotten that idea all wrong. How could Jesus be my friend? He's God! I felt like my job was only to serve Him and love Him, not to befriend Him.

Like many children, I grew up with the dogma that "any friend of yours is a friend of mine," so I've always been pretty inclusive of others. The more the merrier, I said — and I meant it. Now, here I was, friend of Faustina, and she was showing me her best friend, Jesus. Before, I had only known Jesus as Master, Redeemer, Sanctifier, and a dozen other titles. Now, Faustina was asking me to view Jesus under a different title: Friend. I thought back to that core childhood belief, *Any friend of hers is a friend of mine.* By opening my heart to St. Faustina, I learned how to open my heart to Jesus as a friend, a title He had not held in my life before.

As I allowed Jesus to become my friend, that lonely unfillable void I had felt was filled. The only thing that filled the emptiness — the only thing that could possibly fill it — was Christ Himself, in His fullest capacity. Saint Faustina wrote, "O Jesus concealed in the Host, my sweet Master and faithful Friend, how happy my soul is to have such a Friend who always keeps me company. I do not feel lonely even though I am in isolation. Jesus-Host, we know each other — that is enough for me" (*Diary*, 877).

Saint Faustina's *Diary* helped me to understand Him better and understand how He moves in my life. I realized I had been putting Jesus in a box. I needed to accept all of Him, even the parts I did not understand. Once I let Jesus come into my heart — with no restrictions — that void was filled, because my heart longs for everything He is, not just those qualities of His that I can fit into a neat little box and feel safe about.

Saint Faustina found not only comfort in Jesus as her friend, but even happiness and contentment. I had been tiptoeing around the perimeter of the Source, trying to find friendships to fill a void that only Christ Himself could fill. He wanted to be with me in His entirety, and for me to be with Him in my entirety in return, throwing boxes, boundaries, and reservations aside.

Saint Faustina was often scorned by her fellow sisters in the convent, and she felt very much alone. In this age of social

media and busy lives, I feel like so many of us often feel that
way too. Texting and Facebook has taken the place of visiting
each other or making a friendly phone call. It seems like so
often either we cannot make time for loved ones, or our loved
ones cannot make time for us. But St. Faustina speaks to that
directly: "I do not fear at all being abandoned by creatures
because, even if all abandoned me, I would not be alone, for
the Lord is with me" (*Diary*, 1022).

She did not fear the loneliness or abandonment because
she knew she was never truly abandoned. In fact, she was joyful that Christ would have such a special place in her life and
heart that could be filled by no one else.

What Faustina Taught Me About Friendship with Jesus

Jesus is the friend we have always wanted. He says so Himself
in John 15:15: "I have called you friends." These passages
from the *Diary* of St. Faustina highlight some of the qualities
I have found Him to have as my friend.

He is Always There
Do we not thirst for a friend who always answers the phone
when we call? Jesus is always there to lend an ear and His Heart
for our troubles. Jesus said, **"Tell me all, My child, hide
nothing from Me, because My loving Heart, the Heart of
your Best Friend, is listening to you"** (*Diary*, 1486).

He Listens Well
He wants to be a friend with whom we can talk without res-
ervation. He doesn't need anything extraneous. He just says,
"Talk to Me simply, as a friend to a friend" (*Diary*, 1487).
We do not need to be in a certain place at a certain time to talk
to Him; we just need to start talking.

He Speaks the Truth
As a true friend, Jesus will tell us the Truth and asks for the
same in return: **"Let us talk confidentially and frankly, as**

two hearts that love one another do" (*Diary*, 1489). I imagine what "two hearts who love one another" looks like, and that simple picture of communion and purity is exactly what I want to have with Jesus.

He Always Says the Right Thing

Saint Faustina writes about her friendship with Jesus, "In the evening, I went in for a long talk with the Lord Jesus. ... I poured out my whole heart before Him, all my troubles, fears, and apprehensions. Jesus lovingly listened to me and then said, '**Be at peace, My child, I am with you**'" (*Diary*, 1674). Jesus is not one of those friends who does not seem to be listening when we speak or who seems to be more concerned with giving advice or solutions to our problems than being present. Jesus did not brush off St. Faustina's concerns, and He also did not try to fix everything for Faustina; He simply said that He is with her, just like He is with all of us, if we only allow Him to be.

He Knows Exactly What We Need

Jesus wants to shower gifts on us. Like the ultimate spiritual engagement ring, Jesus' graces shine with magnificence, and He only wants us to accept Him: "**If souls would put themselves completely in My care, I Myself would undertake the task of sanctifying them, and I would lavish even greater graces on them**" (*Diary*, 1682). What great love! Jesus will give us everything that we need if we entrust ourselves into His hands.

He Will Never Leave Us

Jesus told St. Faustina, "**Do not fear; I will not leave you alone**" (*Diary*, 881). He is a true friend who will never abandon us, especially in our suffering. Saint Faustina says, "Suffering is the greatest treasure on earth; it purifies the soul. In suffering we learn who is our true friend" (*Diary*, 342). Suffering, like loneliness, is something we may do very much alone unless we allow Jesus to walk with us. He understands the deepest depths of suffering, and will be with us through the lowest points of our lives.

He Appreciates Us

After a tiring day, do we not sometimes just yearn for some sincere words of affirmation? Jesus tells St. Faustina, "**My child, rest on my Heart; I see that you have worked hard in My vineyard**" (*Diary*, 945). Jesus offers us a special place in His Heart. He acknowledges our hard work and calls us His *children*. When I read this entry, it is so easy for me to picture my middle child; she loves to curl up in my lap like a little kitten, her head laid on my chest, content just to hear my heart beat and feel comforted in my arms. If we, like Faustina, are doing his work, Jesus offers us the same protection, praise, and love. How blessed are we!

There are so many more examples of the beautiful type of friend Jesus is; His love and mercy are infinite. Do we trust Him? Can we allow Him to be that friend to us and fill our void? Can we let Him out of the box we've created and allow Him to rule fully in our lives? We all need more of Him; there is never enough Jesus in our lives. I hope that my story helps nudge others into a closer relationship with Jesus and with our saintly brothers and sisters. He and they have so much to offer us. Jesus is waiting for us, expectantly.

An Epilogue

Months after the Confession in which the priest recommended that I read St. Faustina's *Diary*, I went back to Confession with the same priest. After the Sacrament, I reminded him that he had asked me to read the Diary and told him how much that book had helped me. I thanked him profusely, to which he responded, "I never recommended that book, but it is good." To my surprise, he had no recollection of our meeting before, which makes me even more convinced that it was actually God speaking to me through him — we were in a confessional, after all! — telling me to read the *Diary* and discover my first saint friend, Faustina. I thank God for speaking through this priest, even unbeknownst to him, and leading me to my confidante and spiritual sister and, through her, back to the Source and the only One who could fill the void in my heart.

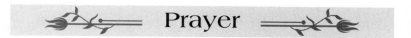

Prayer

Saint Faustina's prayer to the Friend of a lonely heart.

Jesus, Friend of a lonely heart,
You are my haven, You are my peace.
You are my salvation,
You are my serenity in moments of struggle
and amidst an ocean of doubts.
You are the bright ray that lights up the path of my life.
You are everything to a lonely soul.
You understand the soul even though it remains silent.
You know our weaknesses, and like a good physician,
You comfort and heal, sparing us sufferings.
(*Diary*, 247)

CHAPTER 10

The Divine Mercy Novena: A Transformation of Heart

Derya Little

Sin is poison.

Often, we ingest in small amounts, but nowadays a sparkling cordial of poisonous sin is offered as a panacea to all our problems. Gulping it down seems like the best solution, but we become sicker and more miserable. I did not understand sin, and therein lay my problem with a God who could not look upon sin but loved the sinner even unto death. If I was incapable of seeing the truth about myself and accepting that there was indeed something poisoning me, how would I even know to seek an antidote and reach out to a Healer?

I was raised a Muslim in Turkey where sin could be balanced with good deeds. Allah's mercy never made sense, because it seemed everything depended on me. When I lost my faith in Islam after my parents' divorce, the concept of sin completely disappeared from my life. There was no reason for mercy anymore. After years of decadence and emptiness, a Protestant missionary presented a God who declared something sin because it was against our good and the Ultimate Good. That was also the first time I faced the unfathomable distance between my sin and the Ultimate Good for which my heart longed. That was the first time the hollow concept of mercy was filled to the brim.

For many of us, it takes a long time to look in the mirror and realize that Someone should cleanse us of the poison, for we are powerless to save ourselves. It has been 15 years since my Baptism, the ultimate bleach for the soul, and 10 years since my Confirmation into the Church whose shelves are packed with cleansers for all kinds of stains of the soul.

Sin, justice, and mercy are intertwined. Had Adam and Eve stayed perfectly united with God instead of bringing death to the world, then neither would God's justice need to be satisfied, nor would we need His mercy for salvation. But this connection escaped me, because I grew up with a religion where a thing was a sin because Allah said so; therefore, His oft-repeated justice and mercy remained hollow. All we needed was to bow before a master who ruled His subjects with absolute fear and try to gain His favor by earning many brownie points.

Allah is merciful, I was taught. I did not understand mercy, but I understood what happened to those who did not follow the path of Islam. As a woman, that path was especially treacherous, since Muhammed had said that hell was full of women.

At the same time, my concept of justice was no more than the unbridled wrath of an omnipotent deity. Islam was the religion of my childhood. Later I became an atheist and justice became the center of my worldview. But this time, I mistook revenge for justice. Without guidance, these were extremely hard concepts for me to wrap my head around, and it was a great grace when Holy Mother Church finally opened my eyes.

Even after I became a Christian, the brand new understanding of sin and free will was so overwhelming that once again the justice of God who could not look upon sin was all-encompassing for me. Again, mercy remained a question mark in the equation.

Oh how much I am hurt by a soul's distrust! Such a soul professes that I am Holy and Just, but does not believe that I am Mercy and does not trust in My Goodness. Even the devils believe in

My Justice, but do not glorify My Goodness. My Heart rejoices in this title of Mercy (*Diary*, 300).

The intellectual grasp was there, for sure, but unbeknownst to me I needed a personal touch from Heaven for the concept to travel down to my heart and become a burning desire for mercy towards myself and others.

In my husband's mostly brown bachelor home, decorations were meager. One of those rarities was a picture of Jesus touching His Heart where two differently colored rays shot forth. I was a new Catholic and had never heard of this image that was revealed to a simple Polish nun. I had just memorized the St. Michael Prayer, and the painting did not inspire me to take up a new practice. The image that inspired millions did not touch my heart at all, so I shrugged my shoulders and moved on, thinking that Catholics can be weird with their devotions.

Thankfully, St. Faustina would not give up on me. She nudged me to pray the Divine Mercy Novena a couple of years ago, even though I still was not praying the Chaplet. By the grace of God, I remembered to pray all nine days and felt like a refreshing spring breeze went through my soul — but then I let it go again.

Saint Faustina once again rolled her eyes in my general direction and inspired a friend of hers, Michele Faehnle, to send me a little book titled *Divine Mercy for Moms*, in which I read for the first time that even St. Faustina herself was not pleased with the painting. That was the connection I needed, since my shallowness knew no bounds. So a new journey towards a better appreciation of the Divine Mercy devotion started. That was the first day St. Faustina held my hand, as any good friend would, and led me towards our Lord's Sacred Heart, where His love for us burns so bright that He was willing to die for us.

The mercy this Polish nun constantly talked about was not squishy mercy where every injustice and sin is simply forgotten, but precious and Divine Mercy, where justice was satisfied. For one cannot exist without the other. There would be no need for mercy without justice. And without mercy, the darkness of our souls would plunge us into eternal death.

In this perfect harmony, the Divine Mercy Novena beckons us to glare our sin in the eye, knowing that the justice of a perfect and pure God needs to be satisfied, and pray for Christ's mercy to wash over all our inequities. Then, repeat and repeat and repeat again, until you hear "Well done, my good and faithful servant" (Mt 25:21).

Let us look at each day of the novena to get a better glimpse at what the Lord asked of us through St. Faustina:

First Day

"Today bring to Me all mankind, especially all sinners, and immerse them in the ocean of My mercy. In this way you will console Me in the bitter grief into which the loss of souls plunges Me" (*Diary*, 1210).

The problem of evil and its connection to man's sinful nature escaped me for a long time. It was much easier to blame evil men for the world's problems, but one night, the Lord held up a mirror to my soul. I was reading the Grand Inquisitor (a chapter from Dostoyevsky's *Brothers Karamazov*) where a cardinal chastises Jesus for wanting human beings to love Him freely instead of forcing us to follow Him. An image came to my mind of how my selfish decisions, my drunkenness, or my sexual exploitations had hurt countless people and contributed to the intricate web of evil in the world.

This web we weave daily, as one's own sin feeds off those of others and makes more and more people sever their relationship with the only Person that could make them truly happy. The Man who suffered on the Cross sees the brokenness and wants to make all things new. All a soul needs to do is to surrender and accept His mercy. Often, however, as good friends, we need to use our own free will to help others by praying for the lost souls and by offering up our joys and sufferings, even as we witness to the Truth with our lives.

Through His friend, St. Faustina, Christ asks us to pray for the sinners who have become slaves. He is in the business of setting captives free, and He likes us to grab a wire cutter now and then to change people's lives.

Second Day

"Today bring to Me the Souls of Priests and Religious, and immerse them in My unfathomable mercy. It was they who gave me strength to endure My bitter Passion. Through them, as through channels, My mercy flows out upon mankind" (*Diary*, 1212).

All Turkish girls received a talk on modesty and frequently got corrected about their attire. There were no sleeveless shirts or shorts allowed where I grew up. There was always the insinuation that if something unbecoming happened, it was because of women's immodesty, since men had very little control in regard to their sexual behavior. In Islam, sex is a necessity for men.

Then, there is the secular culture, where everything goes as long as it is consensual, because sex is an irresistible urge like hunger or thirst.

As opposed to everything this fallen world offers, the servants of Holy Mother Church beg to differ. The religious, whether they be priests, nuns, monks, sisters, or friars, paint a picture of contrast by their virtue. They offer chastity as a cure to sexual deviance; poverty as a cure to greed and attachment; and obedience as a cure to selfishness, pride, and rebellion. Is it any wonder that they were the ones who gave strength to our Lord during the hardest moments of His Passion?

A faithful religious can be a lifeline for drowning souls. A virtuous life set apart for the Lord stands out like a candle in the dark. But for their light to burn bright, they need prayers. Every mercy we receive through their obedience and ministry should also act as a reminder that they, too, need Divine Mercy to swim against the current of the culture.

It is a good idea not only to remember your own priests, but also all the religious that had an impact on your life through the years. Adopting a seminarian or a novice by learning their names and praying for them regularly would also give them the spiritual support they so need. They have made a sacrifice by standing at the threshold. Offering up daily prayers is the least we can do to buttress their ministry.

Third Day

"Today bring to Me all devout and faithful Souls, and immerse them in the ocean of My mercy. These souls brought me consolation on the Way of the Cross. They were a drop of consolation in the midst of an ocean of bitterness" (*Diary*, 1214).

As I read the *Diary* of St. Faustina, I pictured myself being one of the doubting sisters in her order. My first instinct is always to disbelieve and question. Even after all these years as a Christian, the temptation to wonder whether everything I believe is true or just an elaborate lie visits me more often than I care to admit. Chesterton said, "Merely having an open mind is nothing. The object of opening the mind, as of opening the mouth, is to shut it again on something solid."[14] I imagine the devout and faithful souls our Lord mentions here are those ones who have closed their mouths around the solid food of the Eucharist and refuse to constantly open themselves up to doubt and despair.

Their hearts and minds were oriented towards the Lord sometime in the past. Instead of being influenced by the attacks of the Father of Lies, they remain faithful, like St. Faustina when darkness took a hold of her. She clung to her Lord in prayer and worship, even when she could not even stand up or feel His presence.

However, the closer you get to the Son, the more vicious the spiritual attacks become. Consider St. Anthony of the Desert, who wrestled with demons, or St. John of the Cross, who lived through spiritual darkness. I desire to be one of the devout and faithful souls, but to even slightly resemble one, first I need to learn to lift up the ones who already are. The love of these men and women of God comforted our Lord when there was no comfort to be found, and when I meet them in prayer, maybe I will be more inclined to imitate them in holiness.

Fourth Day

"Today bring to Me those who do not believe in God and those who do not know Me. I was thinking also of them during My bitter Passion, and their future zeal comforted My Heart. Immerse them in the ocean of My mercy" (*Diary*, 1216).

A convert's zeal doesn't diminish easily. A life lived apart from Christ becomes so dark and heavy in comparison to the light yoke of Jesus that holding on to Him is the only thing that keeps misery away. This zeal is not something to boast about, because the convert knows that one is merely a step away from falling into the abyss of a sinful, Christless life.

In His infinite knowledge of the past, the present, and the future, our Lord does not condemn the atheists and the unbelievers, but rejoices in who they might or will become. Consider Saul, who not only oversaw St. Stephen's stoning, but also dragged Christians out of their homes to be tried. Saul became St. Paul. Then there is St. Augustine, St. Dismas, St. Mary Magdalene, and countless others. When the Lord brings you out of the darkness, you know there is nowhere else to go. That is why those who do not believe or know God gave Christ comfort, not agony. When He looks at us, He sees who we can be, like a mother who watches her toddler, constantly falling, stumbling, and crying. She knows that one day that toddler will be doing cartwheels.

When I look back to my own sinful past, I am full of shame and regrets. When the Lord looked at me while I was in the depths of godlessness, He was actually consoled, since

He knew that one day, once the storm passed, my heart would burn for Him.

Every day, I pray for atheists and those who do not know Christ, whether they are friends or family or even complete strangers. How many St. Pauls or St. Augustines are walking around, lost in the darkness of this world? We must plead with the Lord that He will pour out His mercy upon these souls, so they can find their way to Him, sooner rather than later.

Fifth Day

"Today bring to Me the Souls of those who have separated themselves from My Church, and immerse them in the ocean of My mercy. During My bitter Passion they tore at My Body and Heart, that is, My Church. As they return to unity with the Church, My wounds heal, and in this way they alleviate My Passion" (*Diary*, 1218).

The emphasis on unity in the Scriptures is unmistakable. When I first converted, I really had a hard time understanding how all the different Protestant churches reconciled their constant division with our Lord's clear desire for unity. Fallen men ripped apart Christ's Body in their pride and disobedience, but with His mercy, all things can be fixed and made anew. As more and more Christian denominations are giving in to the pressure from secularism, the Church built upon the Rock will remain faithful.

From within and without, the same sinfulness and pride still claw at our Lord's Body. In these times of disunity and confusion, we must pray for the repentance of our separated brethren, so that Christ's Body can be healed and unified once again. With God, all things are possible.

Sixth Day

"Today bring to Me the meek and humble Souls and the souls of little children, and immerse them in My mercy. These souls most closely resemble My Heart. They

strengthened Me during My bitter agony. I saw them as earthly Angels, who would keep vigil at My altars. I pour out upon them whole torrents of grace. Only the humble soul is able to receive my grace. I favor humble souls with My confidence" (*Diary*, 1220).

My 1-year-old giggles breathlessly as she knocks over the thousandth lego tower I built in the last hour. A child's innocence and capacity for joy should make everyone touched by sin envious. Then, once in a while, you see someone so selfless that their mere presence brings comfort, because they have become childlike in their relationship with the Lord. They have become earthly angels.

"It was pride that changed angels into devils; it is humility that makes men as angels," said St. Augustine.[15] Lack of pride is what a child and a humble soul have in common. For ourselves and for all, we must pray ceaselessly that the Lord help us empty ourselves of self-importance, so that our hearts can be filled with Divine Mercy.

Seventh Day

"Today bring to Me the Souls who especially venerate and glorify My Mercy, and immerse them in My mercy. These souls sorrowed most over my Passion and entered most deeply into My spirit. They are living images of My Compassionate Heart. These souls will shine with a special brightness in the next life. Not one of them will go into the fire of hell. I shall particularly defend each one of them at the hour of death" (*Diary*, 1224).

In one of my favorite prayers, St. John Paul II's own prayer to Our Lady, the *Stella Maris* (Star of the Sea), he pleads to Our Lady to "guide seafarers across all dark and stormy seas that they may reach the haven of peace and light prepared in Him who calmed the sea." This is a beautiful and terrible image of our journey on this side of death.

First of all, it is a reminder that we are simply travelers. This is not our home.

Secondly, the seas are constantly raging. Anyone who has seen or understands the darkness of sin is aware of how much we need Christ's mercy. The Church, the ark of salvation, is constantly thrashed about by the waves of the world. The waves are relentless. The night is pitch black. The wind is howling. How easy it is to be obsessed with that storm outside the boat while the Saviour is peacefully taking a nap!

Our Lord reminds St. Faustina and those who listen to her that the only way for any of us to cross the dark and stormy seas is to flee to the One who can command the wind and the sea. Doubt and sin lead us towards desperation and rebellion because the journey seems impossible, but His mercy will lead us to the haven all of us travelers are yearning for. We only need to run to the Lord:

All grace flows from mercy, and the last hour abounds with mercy for us. Let no one doubt concerning the goodness of God; even if a person's sins were as dark as night, God's mercy is stronger than our misery. One thing alone is necessary: that the sinner set ajar the door of his heart, be it ever so little, to let in a ray of God's merciful grace, and then God will do the rest (*Diary*, 1507).

Eighth Day

"Today bring to Me the Souls who are in the prison of Purgatory, and immerse them in the abyss of My mercy. ... Oh, if you only knew the torments they suffer, you would continually offer for them the alms of the spirit and pay off their debt to My justice" (*Diary*, 1226).

Saint Faustina's vision of Purgatory is sobering and hopeful at the same time. After she sees the suffering souls begging for prayer and being refreshed by Our Lady, Star of the Sea, Christ tells her: **"My mercy does not want this, but justice demands it"** (*Diary*, 20). The One without blemish cannot be in perfect union with us while we are still covered in the stains of a sinful past. But remember, despite the cleansing fire, the biggest torment for the souls in Purgatory is their longing for God. It is almost like being parched during a trek through the desert, knowing that you will make it to the other side where life-giving water is waiting for you. At the same time, these souls are perfectly aware that they themselves wandered into the desert knowingly and willingly, and thus must cross the searing sand dunes.

But they are called Holy Souls in Purgatory, because Heaven is within reach. They cannot pray for themselves, so we must constantly pray for them by offering up our sufferings, joys, and works daily, so that they can finally drink from the water that quenches thirst forever.

Ninth Day

"Today bring to Me the souls who have become lukewarm, and immerse them in the abyss of My mercy. These souls wound My Heart most painfully. My soul suffered the most dreadful loathing in the Garden of Olives because of lukewarm souls. They were the reason I cried out: 'Father, take this cup away from Me, if it be Your will.' For them, the last hope of salvation is to flee to My mercy" (*Diary*, 1228).

The last day of the Divine Mercy Novena makes me shiver to my spine, because the lukewarmness is ever a threat to the spiritual life of every Catholic. In the Book of Revelation, the Laodiceans receive a most terrifying warning, "I know your works; I know that you are neither cold nor hot. So, because you are lukewarm, and neither hot nor cold, I will spit you out of my mouth (Rev 3:15-16)."

The world is a deceptive place. The houses we live in, the cars we own, and even the ministries we are involved in open the door to pride; often it happens slowly, without us even noticing, like the proverbial frog being boiled to death. That insatiable hunger for the Lord gives way to worries about finite things until we think we don't really need God anymore. Lukewarmness is the sin of our age.

The danger exists not just for the individual Christian, since the Lord is talking to the angel of a specific church. An entire group of Christians went lukewarm and incurred the wrath of God, not because they apostatized, but because they started to take grace for granted. The grace and mercy received through the Paschal Mystery of Christ became pearls before swine. It is no coincidence that the Lord mentions the same sin on the last day of the novena that He does to the last church addressed in Revelation. He wants to remind us that the race is not over until we are safely home in Heaven. He asks us to stand firm and live a faithful life of joy now that we have received His mercy and all the graces His Church can offer. He asks us to dare to stand up and swim against the current.

Do not be discouraged, however; He also paints one of the most beautiful pictures of His mercy for the Laodiceans: "Behold, I stand at the door and knock. If any one hears my voice and opens the door, I will enter his house and dine with him, and he with me" (Rev 3:20).

Push the door ajar and His mercy will overwhelm all those who heard Him knocking. One drop of His Precious Blood is sufficient to cleanse all the unthinkable sins and unmentionable inequities of humankind.

This is the lesson my friend St. Faustina taught me. Every time I pray the chaplet she whispers in my ear how not to become one of those who filled the Lord's soul with loathing. Her life and visions remind me that I should never presume upon His Mercy without repentance and contrition, but at the same time I should never doubt His mercy by being scrupulous.

Like all saints, St. Faustina takes our hand and hushes our constant inner chatter so that we can hear the Lord knocking on the door day and night.

Will you open the door?

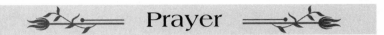

Prayer

Saint Faustina's prayer to the Divine Spirit.

O Divine Spirit, Spirit of truth and of light,
Dwell ever in my soul by Your divine grace.
May Your breath dissipate the darkness,
And in this light may good deeds be multiplied.

O Divine Spirit, Spirit of love and of mercy,
You pour the balm of trust into my heart,
Your grace confirms my soul in good,
Giving it the invincible power of constancy.

O Divine Spirit, Spirit of peace and of joy,
You invigorate my thirsting heart
And pour into it the living fountain of God's love,
Making it intrepid for battle.

O Divine Spirit, my soul's most welcome guest,
For my part, I want to remain faithful to You;
Both in days of joy and in the agony of suffering,
I want always, O Spirit of God, to live in Your presence.

O Divine Spirit, who pervade my whole being
And give me to know Your Divine, Triune Life,
And lead me into the mystery of Your Divine Being,
Initiating me into Your Divine Essence,
Thus united to You, I will live a life without end.
(*Diary*, 1411)

CHAPTER 11

Saint Faustina:
Reminding Me of Who I Am

By Sr. Faustina Maria Pia, SV JMJ

Introduction

My twin sister and I, children of the '80s, born years before St. Faustina was a saint, were often approached and asked what our names were. I'm not sure if they were expecting something along the lines of Cassidy and Kylie or Maddy and Michaela, but our response, "Gertrud and Faustina," always seemed to elicit surprise. We began to expect that look of shock!

Saint Faustina's influence upon me, though, first began years before I existed, in the heart of my mother. At 16 years old, my mother had little faith, and the suffering she had already experienced made her totally indifferent and disinterested in God. Her father had left her family when she was 5, leaving her mother and five older siblings alone and destitute as they faced challenges of poverty and humiliation in Germany following World War II. By the time she was a teen, she noticed a dramatic change in her own mother, who began praying and talking about Jesus. My grandmother's reversion was less than attractive to her suffering children, so when she handed a pamphlet covered with an image of Jesus to her daughter, my mother instantly felt disgust and annoyance. Not wanting to hurt her mother, however, she promised to read it. Months went by until one day the pamphlet with the words "Divine Mercy" — which had been stashed on her bureau — caught her eye again, and she decided to read one page to keep her promise. She opened it, and her eyes fell upon these words of Jesus: **"Let no soul fear to draw near to Me, even though its sins be as scarlet"** (*Diary*, 699).

Immediately tears began streaming down her face. In one instant, Jesus' love poured into her heart, and for the first time, the truth of His unconditional love felt real for *her*. She felt His desire for her to come to Him, to be near Him. She realized that here was this person, Jesus, who loved her so deeply, and wondered why she had been so cold to Him. Getting down on her knees, she repeated over and over again, "Jesus, from this day forward, I want to be your friend. Jesus, from this day forward, I want to be your friend. Jesus, from this day forward, I want to be your friend!" It was a new beginning, and a moment that changed every aspect of her life forever. It was the love of a Father she had never known but always longed for. **"Child, do not run away from your Father; be willing to talk openly with your God of mercy who wants to speak words of pardon and lavish his graces on you. How dear your soul is to Me! I have inscribed your name upon My hand; you are engraved as a deep wound in My Heart"** (*Diary*, 1485). Years later the graces received that night culminated in a miracle of reconciliation with her father shortly before his death. The message of mercy had truly allowed her to taste and believe in a love deeper than any suffering or trial.

The Polish sister pictured on the back of that little pamphlet was to become a treasured friend for life. Her love and devotion to St. Faustina continued to grow over the years, yet she did not name any of her first six children after the holy sister. During her seventh pregnancy, however, when it was discovered that she was carrying twins, my mother had absolute clarity we would be named Gertrud and Faustina; though she had no medical confirmation, she was convinced the twins would be girls. She was right.

In naming me after the Polish sister she had first met at 16 years old, she passed on to me a friendship I, too, needed to grow into. I was born the youngest of eight, and life revolved around my loud and loving family. Everyday phrases included, "Can I please say something without being interrupted?"; "Has anyone seen my other shoe?"; and "We're leaving in one minute!" Amidst the joys and excitement of a full house, I struggled to stand out and find my own identity. There did not seem to be any one thing I was gifted at that others hadn't already mastered. On top of that, it always took me awhile to gather my thoughts and make sense of my feelings, and I began to believe that, unlike my other siblings, I was slow and inept. This did not keep me from building deep friendships in my family and beyond, as I had a natural love for people and a desire to help those who were suffering. After my physician father showed me a model of a human heart in middle school, I decided that I would one day be a cardiologist to serve the sick. Although God had other plans, my love of the human heart has never left me. And through St. Faustina, I have come not only to understand the human heart but also the unique identity and beauty of my own.

Today, the *Diary* of St. Faustina, with my childish signature inside the front cover, is one of my few possessions. It was a gift for my 12th birthday, and the sheer volume of the tome given to me on that day made me feel at once both mature and overwhelmed. I thought I knew who she was from what my parents had told me earlier, but a new aspect of her spiritual life opened up to me as I flipped through the *Diary*. Yes, Jesus was appearing to her, and wanting His merciful love to be revealed to the world through her, but suddenly I was reading about encounters with the devil and trips to Purgatory and hell. No wonder every creak and crack I heard in the hallway then required investigation! It didn't take long for me to surmise this was not a book to read before bed, and eventually, besides a few looks here and there, it sat on my shelf for years.

Getting to know her

Surprisingly, when I was packing for college, St. Faustina's *Diary* made the cut, as I was struck with the thought that I couldn't leave her behind. It was during my years at university that I started to experience more fully the depth of my heart and the tremendous desires I had to love and be loved.

So many nights I would come back to my dorm room after a full day with friends, classes, and all those things that look great and are supposed to bring happiness, and I would feel a painful mix of longing and loneliness, or the restlessness that comes with seeking after superficial things. Often I diverted it through studies or hanging out with friends, but some nights nothing could distract me from the ache I felt inside. I can't remember what prompted me that first time to go to my shelf and pick up the *Diary*, or what particular passage I first took in, but it quickly became my go-to every time that hollowness in my heart surfaced.

No matter what place I opened up the *Diary* to, I always closed it feeling like I had been washed in the truth that I was not alone, and that Jesus cared about me, and even longed for my love. "[Y]ou will feel lonely. **Know then that I want you to unite yourself more closely to Me. I am concerned about every beat of your heart. Every stirring of your love is reflected in My Heart. I thirst for your love**" (*Diary*, 1542).

At the time, I did not know how to pray with Scripture, yet reading what Jesus was saying to St. Faustina, I felt Him speaking to *me*. Without me realizing it, going to Him in the hunger of my heart was the means by which He was teaching me to receive. I discovered that the desire for more — which was with me continually — was a desire for deeper meaning and love. Saint Faustina was stirring my heart to look beyond my to-do lists and social schedule to live my life anchored in eternity, even now. "I know well, O Lord, that You have no need of our works; You demand love. Love, love, and once again, love of God — there is nothing greater in heaven or on earth. The greatest greatness is to love God; true greatness is in loving God; real wisdom is to love God. All that is great and beautiful is in God" (*Diary*, 990).

These periodic, late-night readings with St. Faustina brought not only fresh perspective and hope, but courage. And I needed it. My entire life I had lacked courage. It has always been a real effort for me to be myself, to share my heart, to stand up for what is right, to approach the Lord as I am, truly, and not as someone I thought I should be.

You will not be alone, because I am with you always and everywhere. Near to my Heart, fear nothing. ... What are you afraid of? If you are with Me, who will dare touch you? Nevertheless, I am pleased that you confide your fears to me, My daughter. Speak to Me about everything in a completely simple and human way; by this you give Me great joy (*Diary*, 797).

As much as I loved the relationship between Jesus and St. Faustina, it was not until after I graduated and continued on to nursing school that I recognized myself on the outside looking in. Saint Faustina's mysticism was keeping me at bay. I marveled in disbelief as I read passages in her *Diary* that spoke of visions of Jesus during which He revealed his heart so intimately to her. Meanwhile, the only "visions" I was having revolved around shopping and dating! I couldn't even keep focus for 10 minutes in prayer! And while she was rejoicing in her sufferings, I was so far from that. In fact, I was denying mine or, at best, dragging them along like an unwelcome guest. If we were so different in prayer, I wondered if it could possibly be true that Jesus' words to her were also intended for me.

Vocation

Over the next few years I feared being truly open to the Lord's will for my life. In a way, as only a patron saint of mercy can, she helped me to know with joy and clarity what the Lord was inviting me to through an encounter with His Divine Mercy. Coming home late one night from a clinical rotation at the hospital, I had the grace of courage to share myself with the Lord; how I longed to be happy and yet was miserable and exhausted inside. Without thinking about it, I felt compelled to give Him each of my desires — love and marriage, the type of nurse I wanted to be, where I wanted to live and travel … the list went on and on. I named each desire I experienced in my heart, all the while feeling completely incapable of making my dreams a reality.

I had never been so aware of my own misery and need for God, and in this moment, I heard His voice within me, entrusting me with the desire of His Heart: "I want you for Myself." I knew it was His love, pursuing the gift of my heart, which I had so often overlooked. As I responded "yes" to being totally His, I was flooded with peace and joy. The minute I had finally stopped to catch my breath, He overcame me with His love.

Encountering the real St. Faustina

After a short period of discernment, I entered the Sisters of Life as a postulant. And, as all postulants do, I prayed about what my name as a sister should be. There were so many options that seemed exciting and new, like titles of the Blessed Mother or other saints who had made themselves present to me. Then again, I had hardly begun to explore the virtues — diligence, temperance, or what about magnanimity? Maybe too much of a mouthful! As much fun as it was to speculate and joke, there was a gravity to uncovering my new identity. A part of my heart would always be with St. Faustina, of course, but another part of my heart still felt lost in her shadow.

Towards the end of the year, I was scrambling inside with only a few weeks before I had to submit three choices for my religious name to our Mother Superior — and no one name was sticking. I left for a retreat, hoping for clarity. During the retreat, I noticed an older sister from another congregation smiling at me in the silence as if we knew each other. I politely smiled back, all the while wondering if she was mistaking me for someone else. As the retreat ended and silence was broken, I met her and she said, "Faustina, I remember meeting you when you were 5 years old!" She recounted how a sister in her community had written a book on St. Faustina and would often visit the National Shrine of the Divine Mercy in Stockbridge, Massachusetts. It was there that they met my family and had been struck that the youngest child was named Faustina at a time when the then-Servant of God had few devotees. Over the years these sisters had prayed for me, and now, 20 years later on this retreat, recognized me by my eyes. She then called this other sister, Sr. Sophia, who had written the book on St. Faustina, to come to meet me again.

Sister Sophia greeted me like a long-lost daughter, with a big hug and smile. Handing me her book, I glanced at the title, *The Life of Faustina Kowalska.* I was grateful for the gift, but in my pride, I thought, "I've already met St. Faustina, and I'm not sure I need another book on her." It became evident to me in Sr. Sophia's presence how profoundly she loved St. Faustina and how little I truly appreciated her. Sister Sophia looked at me with joy, and I asked her for prayers, as in a few weeks I would be receiving the habit and my new religious name. With this, her face grew serious, and she grasped my arms, emphasizing every word, "*Don't you dare.*" And she was not alluding to the habit! Her words pierced my heart.

I knew St. Faustina had spoken. It took a chiding word, but it was in the midst of an experience of being known and remembered, almost an experience of being found. Saint Faustina was saying, "If you don't know who you are, I'll remind you!"

Over the next two weeks, I read that book, and it opened my eyes to a St. Faustina I had *not* met. And one I needed to know, before claiming her name as my own.

Here was a red-haired and freckled young woman who, before she entered the convent, people wanted to turn down from nanny jobs because she dressed so fashionably. Who, as a sister, was nicknamed "the lawyer," because she grew passionate when debating and loved to talk with her hands. I was stunned! Social and creative, her sisters loved to sit near her during recreation because she always had something uplifting to say, and her Mother General marveled at the fruitfulness of her work in the garden.

The only St. Faustina I had known was the one who had been asked, under obedience, to write a diary to record all the supernatural phenomena happening in her life. I had little idea of what she was like to be around, the kind of things she enjoyed doing, and, because of that, I had failed to see how human she was. She was no longer distant, but real, and someone like me.

Alongside the naturally attractive aspects of her personality, I began to see her human frailty, too, for the first time. How at times she cared too much about the words and thoughts of others, gave into fears, and was tempted to discouragement. And I also began to see that, far from being annoyed by these frailties, Jesus kept offering His love to her anew.

Saint Faustina would protest to Him how she was unfit for the plan He was revealing for her, saying:

> "You see very well that I am not in good health, that I have no education, that I have no money, that I am an abyss of misery, that I fear contacts with people ... ." And the Lord said to me, **"My daughter, what you have said is true. You are very miserable, and it pleased Me to carry out this work of mercy precisely through you who are nothing but misery itself. Do not fear ... . I will accomplish everything that is lacking in you ... ."** The Lord looked into the depths of my being with great kindness; I thought I would die for joy under that gaze (*Diary*, 881).

And she did fail Him, doubt Him, and was even swayed by a temptation that convinced her that His love and this mission were false (going so far as burning one of her manuscripts). Again, someone not so distant from me! Yet she could meet Him in those very depths where she felt so worthless, and know herself to be loved beyond a doubt! I began to see the whole message of mercy in a new light. This was an invitation for me to step into the truth that my neediness and misery, which had seemed to disqualify me from receiving God's love, actually allowed His Heart to be drawn to me all the more.

Encountering the real me

Saint Faustina's humanity opened a window through which I began to see my own. And I knew Jesus was asking me to take courage. Courage in being more honest with myself, with others, and with Him in the midst of my own neediness and weaknesses, no longer held back by shame and rebellion.

I had grown up hearing how much the Lord loved me, how precious I was to Him, and I believed it, on some level. But those words felt empty to me in the experience of my brokenness, either in my own sinfulness and weakness or how I was treated by others who were likewise broken and limited.

I realized that the parts of me I did not like needed to encounter the Lord's mercy, His unconditional love; otherwise I would end up hating that part of me, or myself entirely. As much as I had tried to cut those parts of myself off, the disdain would remain.

I began to accept the Lord's invitation, and in doing so, I began to accept myself. With every fresh awareness of my own frailties, I made a fresh acknowledgment of my need for the Lord, and stepped into greater dependence on Him. My heart began to breathe more deeply. It wasn't always easy to do this; sometimes I felt like a little girl kicking and screaming, but I could not deny the peace that living in this way brought to my soul. I knew I was *made* to live this kind of openness and vulnerability with Him.

Stepping into this meant entrusting my work to Him in the midst of feeling unprepared despite my best efforts, choosing to believe that He always provides for what He asks, or in making an honest Confession and experiencing a deeper conviction that my sins do hurt Him, but precisely because He loves me so much.

In little and big ways I was coming to know the deep truth of my goodness. The Lord's love is not so much a pitying love, but a love that uncovers the good, or as John Paul II wrote in his encyclical on mercy, *Dives in Misericordia* (*Rich in Mercy*), a love that allows the other to return to the truth about themselves.[16] The Lord in His mercy was taking away the crutches of denial and self-reliance to reveal to me that my dignity was not in what I did or earned but in who I am as His beloved one. **"You would not have been able to bear the magnitude of the love which I have for you if I had revealed it to you fully here on earth. I often give you a glimpse of it, but know that this is only an exceptional grace from Me. My love and mercy knows no bounds"** (*Diary*, 718).

Getting to know the real Jesus

Inside the front cover of the book she gave me that decisive day, Sr. Sophia had inscribed, "May Saint Faustina lead you more deeply to the love of Jesus, the Divine Mercy." Amen to that!

Several years into my religious life, I was struggling to trust the Lord in a particular matter. It was never far from my consciousness, and it seemed the more I prayed about it, the less footing I had. Trust is always about something specific, and this something felt like it was rocking the whole boat of my heart.

In my prayer, I felt Jesus saying, "Trust. Trust Me." Over and over again. Consoled by the fact that St. Faustina herself was almost continually unsure of what she was doing and how to go about it, I turned to the *Diary* of St. Faustina yet again. There I read, as if for the first time, **"The graces of My mercy are drawn by means of one vessel only, and that is — trust. The more a soul trusts, the more it will receive"** (*Diary*, 1578). Why, I wondered? Never had this question so burned on my heart. What is it about trust that so pleases the Lord, that this is the one thing He asks for? Even the short verse Jesus requested to be on every Image of Divine Mercy is simply a prayer of trust — "Jesus, I trust in You." Why not "Jesus, I love You"?

Shortly after, I was praying by bringing to the Lord all the helplessness I felt in the current situation. I still did not understand *why* trust was so pivotal in my relationship with the Lord and was holding out for a clear answer from Him before I would let go of control. If I just knew why, I could consent and then it would be in the comfortable safety of my own understanding. This question of "why trust?"; "why hand this over?" gripped me, and I felt the power of my free will with striking clarity. Suddenly, after months of wrestling, in a moment of sheer grace, it was plain to me that I loved Him, and if He was asking, I wanted to use that power to trust even if I didn't understand. He wanted me to choose Him over myself and take Him for His word — regardless of *hows* and *whys*. My whole heart swelled with a strong desire simply to trust Jesus, whatever it entailed, so that I could receive His love as He desires me to — to give Him that joy. What did follow was a surprising, equally strong desire that hearts everywhere would also trust Him, so that His love would be received all over the world more and more! I realized He was actually teaching me who He was — that He was deeply good. He knew what I needed, and in requiring this openness of letting go, He received the freedom to act in my life.

Then, these words came over my heart: *Write the Litany of Trust.* All I could think of was the Litany of Humility, and so, using the structure of that prayer, I simply wrote what flowed from my heart. For about a year I prayed it privately, but as the Year of Mercy approached, I shared it with others, knowing it was not just for me.

The simplest way I can explain the prayer is that oftentimes at the end of the day, we feel a tension, a restlessness or agitation inside. Sometimes we may feel this at the beginning of the day, or the middle, or all day! Small or large, these tensions all too often stem from two lies that block our hearts from the Lord: that God is not good, or that I am not good. And these are precisely the points where Jesus so desires that we trust, so His mercy can enter and bring new life there. This prayer fights against these falsehoods, saying, "I will not live based off of those lies, but instead will keep my heart open in trust." **"The flames of mercy are burning Me — clamoring to be spent; I want to keep pouring them out upon souls; souls just don't want to believe in My goodness"** (*Diary*, 177).

In choosing to trust the Lord, especially at a time when I did not feel His presence, I found His love poured into my heart. He has shown Himself faithful and trustworthy, not only in bringing the situation I was struggling with to a resolution, but far more, in revealing Himself to me as the One who is worth everything.

All these years after her death, I am grateful that St. Faustina continues to share herself in this mission of mercy and, in befriending me, has drawn my own heart into it. Whether someone has been in the trenches of the culture of death and is desperate to know their own goodness, or helping someone to take courage to seek forgiveness in the Sacraments, or being with those who are on the brink of depending on Jesus in a painful situation, I long to share the simple message of trusting God's goodness in a way people can live and believe in their everyday lives.

Now when I share my name with people I meet, there is still a surprise — but often it is a delight that accompanies the remembrance of a friend. Yes, I am named for *her*!

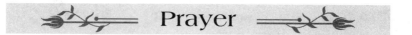

Prayer

Litany of Trust
Sr. Faustina Maria Pia, SV

From the belief that I have to earn Your love
Deliver me, Jesus.
From the fear that I am unlovable **Deliver me, Jesus.**
From the false security that I have what it takes
Deliver me, Jesus.
From the fear that trusting You will leave me more
destitute **Deliver me, Jesus.**
From all suspicion of Your words and promises
Deliver me, Jesus.
From the rebellion against childlike dependency on You
Deliver me, Jesus.
From refusals and reluctances in accepting Your will
Deliver me, Jesus.
From anxiety about the future **Deliver me, Jesus.**
From resentment or excessive preoccupation with the
past **Deliver me, Jesus.**
From restless self-seeking in the present moment
Deliver me, Jesus.
From disbelief in Your love and presence
Deliver me, Jesus.
From the fear of being asked to give more than I have
Deliver me, Jesus.
From the belief that my life has no meaning or worth
Deliver me, Jesus.
From the fear of what love demands **Deliver me, Jesus.**
From discouragement **Deliver me, Jesus.**

That You are continually holding me, sustaining me,
  loving me **Jesus, I trust in You.**
That Your love goes deeper than my sins and failings,
  and transforms me **Jesus, I trust in You.**
That not knowing what tomorrow brings is an invitation
  to lean on You **Jesus, I trust in You.**
That You are with me in my suffering
  Jesus, I trust in You.
That my suffering, united to Your own, will bear fruit in
  this life and the next **Jesus, I trust in You.**
That You will not leave me orphaned, that You are
  present in Your Church **Jesus, I trust in You.**
That Your plan is better than anything else
  Jesus, I trust in You.
That You always hear me and in Your goodness always
  respond to me **Jesus, I trust in You.**
That You give me the grace to accept forgiveness and to
  forgive others **Jesus, I trust in You.**
That You give me all the strength I need for what is
  asked **Jesus, I trust in You.**
That my life is a gift **Jesus, I trust in You.**
That You will teach me to trust You
  Jesus, I trust in You.
That You are my Lord and my God
  Jesus, I trust in You.
That I am Your beloved one **Jesus, I trust in You.**

References

Vatican II, *Lumen Gentium* (*Dogmatic Consitution on the Church*), November 18, 1965, http://www.vatican.va/archive/hist_councils/ii_vatican_council/documents/vat-ii_const_19641121_lumen-gentium_en.html.

M. Elzbieta Siepak, OLM, *A Gift from God for Our Times: The Life and Mission of Saint Faustina* (Krakow, PL: Misericordia Publications, 2007).

Eva Czaczkowska, *Faustina the Mystic and Her Message* (Stockbridge, MA: Marian Press, 2007).

Biographies of Contributing Authors

Michele Faehnle is a Catholic author, speaker, registered nurse, wife, and mother. Michele earned a bachelor of science degree (cum laude) in nursing from Franciscan University of Steubenville in 1999 and currently works as a school nurse at St. Andrew School in Upper Arlington. She is the co-author of the bestselling, award-winning *Divine Mercy for Moms* and *The Friendship Project.* She is also the co-director of the Columbus Catholic Women's Conference, the largest Catholic Women's Conference in the United States, with over 3500 attendees each year. She blogs at divinemercyformoms.com, is a contributor to CatholicMom.com, and writes for *Today's Catholic Teacher* magazine. Michele has spoken to several women's groups and national conferences, including presentations at the National Shrine of The Divine Mercy on Divine Mercy Sunday. She speaks on St. Faustina and the Divine Mercy devotion, technology and our children, and the importance of spiritual friendships. She and her husband, Matthew, have four children and live in Columbus, Ohio.

Emily Jaminet is a Catholic author, speaker, radio personality, wife, and mother of seven children. She co-authored the award-winning book *Divine Mercy for Moms*, as well as *The Friendship Project*, both published by Ave Maria Press. She is currently the media and evangelization coordinator for the Sacred Heart Enthronement Network and writes for the *Catholic Digest*. She serves on the leadership team of the Columbus Catholic Women's Conference and blogs at divinemercyformoms.com, www.emilyjaminet.com, and is a contributor to CatholicMom.com. Emily earned a bachelor's degree in mental health and human services from the Franciscan University of Steubenville. She offers a daily segment called "A Mother's Moment" on St. Gabriel Catholic Radio and Mater Dei Radio. She and her husband live in Columbus, Ohio, with their seven children.

Allison Gingras shares the beauty of the Catholic Faith with honesty, laughter, and relatable examples from everyday, ordinary life: ReconciledToYou.com. She has created the Stay Connected Journals for Catholic Women (Our Sunday Visitor), which includes her book, The Gift of Invitation: 7 Ways Jesus Invites Us into a Life of Grace. Allison is a contributing author to Road Signs for Catholic Teens (Our Sunday Visitor) and Catholic Mom's Prayer Companion (Ave Maria Press). Her podcast A Seeking Heart with Allison Gingras is distributed through BreadboxMedia.com. Allison offers retreats and inspirational talks on the Grace Trifecta, Mary as Model of a Worry-Free Life; Seeking the Peace of Forgiveness, and Faith in the Everyday! Allison is blessed to work for WINE: Women In the New Evangelization. She contributes articles to CatholicVineyard.com, CatholicMom.com, Pauline Cooperators, Catholic Stand, and CatholicSistas.

Elizabeth Ficocelli is an inspirational Catholic speaker for international audiences at conferences, parishes, schools, retreats, and events. She can be seen and heard frequently on Catholic radio and television, including guest hosting live national radio programs such as "Catholic Connection and

Kresta in the Afternoon." Elizabeth also hosts her own program, "Answering the Call," on St. Gabriel Catholic Radio AM 820, in which she interviews priests, deacons, and religious about their spiritual journeys. In addition to her speaking and media work, Elizabeth is a best-selling, award-winning author of 15 books for adults and young people, as well as numerous Catholic magazine articles. She and her husband of 34 years have four boys and reside in Columbus, Ohio.

Brooke Taylor is a speaker, writer, and radio personality. As the host of the popular podcast "Good Things Radio," Brooke shares her heart and vision of hope in Jesus Christ with audiences everywhere. Brooke's 20-year media career includes serving as co-host of the "Family Friendly Morning Show" on 95.5 "The Fish" out of Cleveland, Ohio. Her travels also include leading pilgrimages to the Holy Land and Italy. As a nationally recognized speaker, she loves sharing her heart with audiences on topics such as faith, adoption, parenting special needs children, community, joy, and the power of one voice. Brooke and her husband, Jim, are busy raising their five children: four sons and a daughter they adopted from Poland. Visit www.BrookeTaylor.us for more information.

Kaitlyn Clare Mason is the founder of Mary Garden Showers, a ministry sharing Christ's mercy with women and families in crisis pregnancies through baby showers for women choosing to directly parent, and blessing showers for women choosing adoption. Author, songwriter, and homesteader-in-training, she is blessed to be a wife and mother of four children. She writes to help you trust and serve at your full capacity at kaitlynclaremason.com.

Lori Ubowski is a Catholic musician, music director, blogger, and the author of *Side by Side: A Catholic Mother-Daughter Journal* (Ave Maria Press, 2018). She tours the United States sharing the Gospel through her music ministry, "Out of Darkness," and she and her husband are blessed to lead music and provide talks for retreats, youth conferences, Adoration, liturgies, worship-leader training, and concert-style worship events throughout the country.

Chiara Finaldi is a wife, mother of seven, and blogger from London, England. She grew up on the Mediterranean island of Sicily in Italy and moved to England after marrying in 1999. She blogs at catholicpearl.blogspot.com and founded in 2015 an international online community through Facebook called "Catholic Mothers," which now has over 2,500 members. Chiara is the organizer of the UK Catholic Mothers' Conference, the Catholic Mother Daughter Conference and author of the Catholic Mothers' Planner 2019. She also created the Catholic Mothers online shop that brings to England new, exciting Catholic products previously unavailable in the UK and Europe. She enjoys "wasting" time with her husband and their seven children, and delights in the gift of an enormous extended family, where music and good food is never lacking. She finds joy in painting and constantly learning new crafts and artistic skills.

Lis Luwia is the founder of DioceseEvents.com where she shares Catholic events throughout the USA to help bring the communion of saints into greater community. She also runs the popular VIP email: "Your Catholic Insider" where she shares exciting Catholic news, liturgical living ideas, coupons, and freebies, specifically for Catholic moms and educators of Catholic kids. Lis also founded CatholicMommyBlogs.com which is where "Your Catholic Insider" lives. Lis is also the author of several prayer journals including *My Catholic Prayer Journal* and *Our Lady of Sorrows: A Catholic Meditation & Prayer Journal*. Lis, her husband, and three daughters attend Catholic events, worship, and live in the Midwest.

Derya Little was born and raised in Muslim Turkey. She rejected her family's Islamic faith and became an atheist after her parents' divorce. During her stormy adolescence, she tried to convince a Christian that there is no God but was converted to Christ instead. During her doctoral studies in England, she entered the Catholic Church. Nowadays, she lives in a small town with her husband and four children, enjoying coffee, kissing booboos, and writing about the worlds she imagined. She can be found at deryalittle.com and on social media.

Sister Faustina Maria Pia, SV, originally from Connecticut, is a twin and the youngest of eight children. She studied psychology at Franciscan University of Steubenville, and later went on to nursing school, where she discovered the Lord's invitation to be consecrated to Him. She entered the Sisters of Life in 2009. The Sisters of Life, based out of New York, serve the most vulnerable, proclaiming with their lives the sacred dignity of every human life — especially those whose lives are hidden, weak, or wounded. Their missions include caring for vulnerable pregnant women and their unborn children; fostering a culture of life through evangelization; inviting those suffering after abortion into Jesus' healing mercy; a mission of accompaniment for college students; retreat works; and upholding the beauty of marriage and family life. Sister Faustina has served her sisters in the postulant formation program and is currently the assistant to the vocation director. She loves the mountains and all things rustic, but most of all, bringing to others the knowledge of the Merciful Heart of Jesus. Several years ago, while struggling with the Lord over the need for trust, she felt inspired to write the Litany of Trust, which has been an instrument of grace and deepened trust for countless souls.

Our Friend Faustina Themes & Study Guide Questions

Introduction:

"I feel certain that my mission will not come to an end upon my death, but will begin. O doubting souls, I will draw aside for you the veils of heaven to convince you of God's goodness, so that you will no longer continue to wound with your distrust the sweetest Heart of Jesus" (*Diary*, 281).

1. What do you hope to get out of this study?

2. Had you heard of St. Faustina before you picked up this book? What are your thoughts about this saint?

3. Michele discussed the process of writing this book and getting the proposal in on time. Are there times in your life when you, too, have seen God align your life so you have been able to accomplish all you needed to do?

4. Can you think of a time when you doubted God's plan for you in your life and later thanked Him for the path He gave you?

5. What has held you back from trusting the Heart of Jesus?

CHAPTER 1

Tapped on the Shoulder by St. Faustina
(Michele Faehnle)

Theme: Joining our will to the will of God

"Now I understand well that what unites our soul more closely to God is self-denial; that is, joining our will to the will of God" (*Diary*, 462).

"From today on, I do the Will of God everywhere, always, and in everything" (*Diary*, 374).

1. Looking back over this chapter, what was your primary takeaway?

2. This book is filled with wonderful accounts of devotion to St. Faustina. As Lumen Gentium says, the friendship of the saints is not "weakened or interrupted" by their death, but instead, strengthened by the bonds of our faith and "communication of spiritual goods." Have you ever experienced a saint as a friend in your life? Sometimes saints seem to choose us, but other times, they're just waiting for our invitation. Is there a particular saint you would like to invite to walk alongside you at this time in your life?

3. After reading the brief biography of St. Faustina is there an aspect of her upbringing that you find remarkable or inspiring?

4. Saint Faustina had only two years of formal education, yet Jesus asked her to undertake the mission of spreading this great devotion. Do you ever feel unqualified to do the work that God is asking of you? In what ways has the Lord made up for what you lack?

5. "From today on, I do the Will of God everywhere, always, and in everything" (*Diary*, 374). Because of

There is a need to recommit to offering my whole life

this entry, Michele shared that she has made it a priority each morning to say this prayer when she grabs her coffee: "Dear Lord, conform my will to Yours and do not let my will get in the way of Yours." This powerful supplication each morning has brought about drastic change in her life. Have you considered giving God your will? What is holding you back?

CHAPTER 2

Life Lessons Learned from Faustina
(Emily Jaminet)

Theme: Living a life of mercy

"I am giving you three ways of exercising mercy towards your neighbor: the first — by deed, the second — by word, the third — by prayer. In these three degrees is contained the fullness of mercy, and it is an unquestionable proof of love for Me. By this means a soul glorifies and pays reverence to My mercy" (*Diary*, 742).

1. Looking back over this chapter, what was your primary takeaway?

2. Which way of exercising mercy towards others do you feel most comfortable performing? Do you prefer to serve others through your deeds, by your words, or by prayers? — *mostly done out of convenience*

   would like opportunities time

3. In the *Diary* (318), St. Faustina writes: "I often feel God's presence after Holy Communion in a special and tangible way. I know God is in my heart. And the fact that I feel Him in my heart does not interfere with my duties." Do you sometimes feel Christ's presence after receiving Him in the Eucharist? Do you picture Christ joining you at work, at home, or out with friends?

4. Jesus speaks to St. Faustina in the *Diary*, "[W]ith **childlike simplicity talk to Me about everything, for My ears and heart are inclined towards you, and your words are dear to Me**" (*Diary*, 921). Where do you feel most comfortable talking to Jesus? How do you find time to talk to Him throughout your day? What do you do (or can you do) to remind yourself that you are never alone or abandoned?

5. How do you describe the value of doing meaningful deeds for others? Has a friend of family member introduced you or have you been involved in a great service that has brought meaning to your life?

6. Emily shared the powerful story of praying the Chaplet of Divine Mercy at the bedside of a sick person. We read the importance of praying for those who are sick and dying in the *Diary*: "**At the hour of their death, I defend as My own glory every soul that will say this chaplet; or when others say it for a dying person, the pardon is the same. When this chaplet is said by the bedside of a dying person, God's anger is placated, unfathomable mercy envelops the soul, and the very depths of My tender mercy are moved for the sake of the sorrowful Passion of My Son**" (*Diary*, 811). Have you considered praying the Chaplet with someone who is sick or dying? What opportunities do you have to do this?

✳️Holy Name —during Lent every Sun. pray the chaplet and benediction

CHAPTER 3

A Life Intertwined with
My Friend Faustina
(Allison Gingras)

Theme: Developing an intimate relationship
with Jesus through Adoration of the
Blessed Sacrament

"That same day, when I was in church waiting for confession, I saw the same rays issuing from the monstrance and spreading throughout the church. This lasted all through the service. After the Benediction, [the rays shone out] to both sides and returned again to the monstrance. Their appearance was bright and transparent like crystal. I asked Jesus that He deign to light the fire of His love in all souls that were cold. Beneath these rays a heart will grow warm even if it were like a block of ice; even if it were hard as a rock, it will crumble into dust" (*Diary*, 370).

1. Looking back over this chapter, what was your primary takeaway?

2. Do you have someone to act as a spiritual director in your life? Saint Faustina's was instrumental in helping her to discern and to accomplish important missions in her life. How do you think a spiritual director could be a blessing to you?

3. Saint Faustina experienced an intimate relationship with Jesus, which included time in Adoration of the Blessed Sacrament. In the noise and bustle of everyday life, it can be a Herculean task to hear Jesus speaking to our hearts. How can you arrange your calendar to ensure that you have at least 15 minutes a week to visit with the Lord in the Eucharist?

4. What attention do you give to the 3 o'clock Hour of Great Mercy each day? How often do you recite the Divine Mercy Chaplet?

5. For Allison, St. Faustina was instrumental in helping her through the adoption process for her daughter Faith. Have you had a similar experience with a heavenly helper, when you feel either Faustina or another saint has helped you navigate a challenge, change, or triumph in your life?

CHAPTER 4

My Miracle of Mercy
(Elizabeth Ficocelli)

Theme: Experiencing mercy in Confession

"My daughter, just as you prepare in My presence, so also you make your confession before Me. The person of the priest is, for Me, only a screen. Never analyze what sort of a priest it is that I am making use of; open your soul in confession as you would to Me, and I will fill it with My light" (*Diary*, 1725).

1. Looking back over this chapter, what was your primary takeaway?

2. Elizabeth shared about some of her own personal struggles related to her family life. Are there areas in your life where you need to seek forgiveness? How can growing in God's trust and the Sacrament of Confession go together?

3. Elizabeth wrote: "I find it ironic that I was so attracted to this message of God's unconditional forgiveness when at the same time I had been struggling for years with the concept of a Catholic Confession." If this Sacrament is so powerful, why do you think so many

Catholics struggle with going to Confession? Have you struggled with this Sacrament? What advice do you have for others who may be doubtful about or fearful of going to Confession?

CHAPTER 5

My Soul Sister Faustina
(Brooke Taylor)

Theme: Jesus is with us in our sufferings

"Jesus looked at me kindly and said, '**My daughter, do not be afraid of sufferings: I am with you**'" (*Diary*, 151).

"My Jesus, support me when difficult and stormy days come, days of testing, days of ordeal … . Sustain me, Jesus, and give me strength to bear suffering. Set a guard upon my lips that they may address no word of complaint to creatures. Your most merciful Heart is all my hope" (*Diary*, 1065).

1. Looking back over this chapter, what was your primary takeaway?

2. In this chapter, Brooke mentions the faith-based movie *Nine Days that Changed the World*. What movie have you seen that impacted your life or encouraged you to take a leap of faith?

3. Brooke shares with us in this chapter, "[S]pending time with my friend St. Faustina taught me the value of quiet contemplation. … The pre-dawn visits to the Adoration chapel gave me endurance and peace." What is the hardest thing about finding time to pray? What have you tried that works? What doesn't work?

4. Brooke shared the simple phrase, "Worry consumed me" regarding her adoption and pregnancy occurring at the same time. Jesus shared with St. Faustina in the *Diary*, "**Do as much as is in your power,**

and do not worry about the rest. These difficulties prove that this work is Mine" (*Diary*, 1295). Jesus tells St. Faustina over and over again in the *Diary*, "**Do not worry**" and "**Fear nothing.**" Have you ever been overwhelmed by a worry or fear that needed Christ's intervention or help? How can we learn to trust and not worry?

5. Brooke had her daughter's name "Karolina" pop into her head while on the treadmill, before she had met her or knew her given name. This moment was more than a coincidence. It was a holy confirmation or God-incidence. If you have had a moment like this, talk a bit about the events that led up to it. What effect did it have on your life, particularly your prayer life?

6. Faustina devoted her life to "attending *well.*" Her interior thoughts reveal a soul in perpetual union with our Lord. How can you learn to focus more on the Lord?

CHAPTER 6

Gardens of Mercy

(Kaitlyn Mason)

Theme: Marian Consecration

"Smiling at me [Mary] said to me, '*My Daughter, at God's command I am to be, in a special and exclusive way your Mother: but I desire that you, too, in a special way, be My child*'" (*Diary*, 1414).

1. Looking back over this chapter, what was your primary takeaway?

2. Saint Faustina had a strong devotion to the Blessed Mother. She wrote in her *Diary*, "I am quite at peace, close to Her Immaculate Heart" (*Diary*, 1097). What

is your relationship like with the Blessed Mother? Does she have a role in your life?

3. In this chapter, Kaitlyn talks about harboring some "Marian discomfort," and how, by "leaning in" to this discomfort, she realized that Mary is actually there to comfort and to guide us to Christ. Have you ever experienced discomfort in your own spiritual journey? What can we do to "lean in" and learn more when we are experiencing doubt or confusion in our personal faith?

4. In this chapter, we learned about how Mary Garden Showers is encouraging new lives to be brought into the world, creating a new kind of garden for Mary. There are many beautiful acts of mercy that start out as seeds, and with time and prayer, they can bloom and grow into fields of flowers for our Merciful Mother. What new garden might God be calling you to plant and nurture for Mary?

5. Have you considered consecrating yourself to Mary? (Father Michael Gaitley's book *33 Days to Morning Glory* might be a great place to start.) If you've already completed a Marian Consecration, what impact has this had on your personal and family life so far?

CHAPTER 7

Mercy Unseen
(Lori Ubowski)

Theme: Surrender in times of
difficulty and despair

"**Do not be discouraged by the difficulties you encounter in proclaiming My mercy. These difficulties that affect you so painfully are needed for your sanctification and as evidence that this work is Mine**" (*Diary*, 1142).

1. "After such sufferings the soul finds itself in a state of great purity and very close to God. But I should add that during these spiritual torments it is close to God, but it is blind. The soul's vision is plunged into darkness, and though God is nearer than ever to the soul which is suffering, the whole secret consists in the fact that it knows nothing of this" (*Diary*, 109). Have you ever felt God was close to you when life was the most challenging?

2. Lori subtitled part of her chapter: **Surrender= Trust**. Can you relate to Lori's spiritual conclusion? Have you had to surrender a major trouble or difficulty like the one Lori mentioned? When have you needed to surrender sickness, financial troubles, or other personal difficulties to the Lord? How can we grow in moments like these?

3. Lori wrote about how God works through people. We are His Body, His means of expressing love to others. In this chapter, we read the story of how two parishes joined together and presented Adam and Lori with the check to help finance their first music album. Do you think this gesture would have had the same impact if their family not gone through the difficult time with the destruction of their rental home?

4. In the *Diary*, we read the words of Jesus to St. Faustina, "**My child you are My delight, you are the comfort of My Heart. I grant you as many graces as you can hold. As often as you want to make Me happy, speak to the world about My great and unfathomable mercy**" (*Diary*, 164). Do you have a story of how God's mercy has impacted your life? Have you experienced a healing, a special grace or a miracle that lead you to a deepening of your faith?

CHAPTER 8
Language of the Soul
(Chiara Finaldi)

Theme: Serving Christ through Serving Others

"Once, when I returned to my cell, I was so tired that I had to rest a moment before I started to undress, and when I was already undressed, one of the sisters asked me to fetch her some hot water. Although I was tired, I dressed quickly and brought her the water she wanted, even though it was quite a long walk from the cell to the kitchen, and the mud was ankle-deep. When I re-entered my cell, I saw the ciborium with the Blessed Sacrament, and I heard this voice, '**Take this ciborium and bring it to the tabernacle**.' I hesitated at first, but when I approached and touched it, I heard these words, '**Approach each of the sisters with the same love with which you approach Me; and whatever you do for them, you do it for Me**.' A moment later, I saw that I was alone" (*Diary*, 285).

1. Looking back over this chapter, what was your primary takeaway?

2. Chiara writes about St. Faustina, "As I read about the life of this young girl originally named Helen Kowalska, I found the ordinary life of an ordinary girl, who had nothing by the world's standards. This was a girl with a very common surname and a poor background, a girl who could hardly read and write in her own language. The more I looked for greatness in her, the more I discovered poverty, weakness, and humanity." How do you believe God can (or does) work in your ordinary life?

3. Chiara said, "Why could I not be more like St. Faustina? Why was I rarely able to rest in the Lord

in my struggles?" How has the life of St. Faustina (or other saints) inspired you to turn your struggles over to Christ and rest in Him?

4. Christ desires us to serve others: our family, friends, and greater community. How has your faith inspired you to serve others? How did Chiara's change of heart and perspective help her?

5. Chiara felt called to plan a conference for Catholic mothers in England. Although she felt ill equipped to take on such a challenge, she trusted in Jesus; the planning, although tiring, was never difficult, and "every step was already laid out and prepared ahead of time for me." Describe a time when you experienced taking on a big task for God where He paved the way for it to happen, even though you felt you could not do the job?

6. In this chapter, we read how Chiara was not drawn to the image or devotion to Divine Mercy and quickly passed on anything she received about it to others. What has been your experience with this devotion? Is it new to you, or a treasured source of grace in your life?

CHAPTER 9
Talk to Me, Friend to Friend: St. Faustina's Cure for Loneliness
(Lis Luwia)

Theme: Friendship with the saints
leads us to Jesus

"Jesus, Friend of a lonely heart, You are my haven, You are my peace. You are my salvation, You are my serenity in moments of struggle and amidst an ocean of doubts. You are the bright

ray that lights up the path of my life. You are everything to a
lonely soul. You understand the soul even though it remains
silent. You know our weaknesses and You comfort and heal,
sparing us sufferings" (*Diary*, 247).

1. Looking back over this chapter, what was your primary takeaway?

2. Have you ever felt lonely? If so, has it brought you closer to God or pulled you further away from Him?

3. In this chapter, Lis shared about the void in her life. She wrote, "My wonderful children could not fill the void, blogging could not fill the void, online friendships had not filled the void, and now these fantastic friendships I was building could not fill the void." She realized she could only be nourished by developing a meaningful relationship with God. Can you relate to Lis' journey? Have you felt lonely and longed for a friend and realized that you were also longing for Christ?

4. Lis wrote, "I asked Jesus to lead me to more saint friends. I would read about their lives, celebrate their feast days, and pray to them during the day. They became my own little posse, my support system and confidants. But I still wanted more. I asked my friend Faustina what I should do. Like a good friend who knows exactly what to do, she led me right to the Source: I slowly began to befriend Jesus." How can you relate to this passage? Have you taken time out to get to know the lives of the saints? How have they drawn you closer to Christ?

5. At the end of this chapter, Lis shares seven themes from the *Diary* of St. Faustina. Turn back to page 124 and share which theme spoke to you.

CHAPTER 10

The Divine Mercy Novena: A Transformation of Heart

(Derya Little)

Theme: Mercy and justice

"Today I am sending you with My mercy to the people of the whole world. I do not want to punish aching mankind, but I desire to heal it, pressing it to My Merciful Heart. I use punishment when they themselves force Me to do so; My hand is reluctant to hold the sword of justice. Before the Day of Justice I am sending the Day of Mercy" (*Diary*, 1588).

1. Looking back over this chapter, what was your primary takeaway?

2. "Sin is poison." Can you relate to that statement? How is sin poison?

3. Have you ever prayed the Divine Mercy Novena? The most popular time to pray it is nine days before Divine Mercy Sunday, to prepare for the feast day; however, it can be prayed any time during the year. At the National Shrine of The Divine Mercy, the Chaplet of Divine Mercy Novena is recited perpetually at the Hour of Great Mercy — the 3 o'clock hour. What has been your experience praying the Divine Mercy Novena?

4. Each day of the novena prays for a different intention. Have you thought to pray for each of these groups before? Which one spoke to you most powerfully?

5. After reading more about each aspect of the novena, review and discuss the final Scripture: "Behold, I stand at the door and knock. If anyone hears my voice and opens the door, I will enter his house and dine with him, and he with me" (Rev 3:20). How can

we welcome Christ into our heart and pray for those
who need us?

CHAPTER 11

Saint Faustina:
Reminding Me of Who I Am

(Sr. Faustina Maria Pia, SV)

Theme: Trust

**"The graces of My mercy are drawn by means of one vessel
only, and that is — trust. The more a soul trusts, the more
it will receive"** (*Diary*, 1578).

1. Looking back over this chapter, what was your primary takeaway?

2. Sister Faustina Pia shares about her grandmother's
    and then her mother's conversion and the impact of
    that on her life. How has the faith of your relatives
    impacted you?

3. Jesus says to St. Faustina in the *Diary*, **"Child, do
    not run away from your Father; be willing to
    talk openly with your God of mercy who wants
    to speak words of pardon and lavish his graces
    on you. How dear your soul is to Me! I have
    inscribed your name upon my My hand; you are
    engraved as a deep wound in My Heart"** (*Diary*,
    1485). How do we choose to run away from God
    the Father? Does talking to God come easily for you?

4. Sister Faustina Pia wrote about her experience with
    the *Diary* while she was in college: "I did not know
    how to pray with Scripture, and yet reading what Jesus
    was saying to St. Faustina, I felt Him speaking to *me*.
    Without me realizing it, going to Him in the hunger

of my heart was the means by which He was teaching me to receive." Describe a time that a spiritual book impacted your life and brought you closer to Christ?

5. Sister Faustina Pia shared in this chapter how she knew she was called to be a Sister of Life: "I felt compelled to give Him each of my desires and from this I was able to understand that God was calling me to a religious vocation." Why do we hesitate to give God our greatest desires? Have you prayed Sr. Faustina Pia's Litany of Trust? What spoke to you from that prayer?

Endnotes

Introduction

[1] Pope John Paul II, Homily for the Canonization of Sr. Maria Faustina Kowalska, April 30, 2000, http://w2.vatican.va/content/john-paul-ii/en/homilies/2000/documents/hf_jp-ii_hom_20000430_faustina.html, no. 8.

Chapter 1

[2] Vatican II, *Lumen Gentium* (*Dogmatic Constitution On the Church*), November 21, 1964, http://www.vatican.va/archive/hist_councils/ii_vatican_council/documents/vat-ii_const_19641121_lumen-gentium_en.html.

[3] M. Elzbieta Siepak, OLM, *A Gift from God for Our Times: The Life and Mission of Saint Faustina* (Krakow, PL: Misericordia Publications, 2007), 35.

[4] Ewa K. Czaczkowska, *Faustina the Mystic and Her Message* (Stockbridge, MA: Marian Press, 2014), 244.

[5] Siepak, *Gift from God for Our Times*, 111-112.

[6] Michele Faehnle and Emily Jaminet, *Divine Mercy for Moms: Sharing the Lessons of St. Faustina* (Notre Dame, IN: Ave Maria Press, 2015).

[7] Michael Gaitley, MIC, *33 Days to Morning Glory: A Do-It-Yourself Retreat in Preparation for Marian Consecration* (Stockbridge, MA: Marian Press, 2011).

Chapter 2

[8] Grzegorz Gorny and Janusz Rosikon, *Trust: In Saint Faustina's Footsteps* (San Francisco: Ignatius Press, 2014), 149.

Chapter 3

[9] Susan Tassone, *St. Faustina Prayer Book for Adoration* (Huntington, IN: Our Sunday Visitor, 2018).

[10] Sr. Sophia Michalenko, CMGT, *The Life of Faustina Kowalska: The Authorized Biography* (Ann Arbor, MI: Charis Books, 1999), 22.

Chapter 4

[11] Elizabeth Ficocelli, "Confessions of a Catholic Convert," *St. Anthony's Messenger*, March 2003.

Chapter 5

[12] Pope John Paul II, Homily at the Mass for the Canonization of Sr. Maria Faustina Kowalksa, no. 8.

Chapter 6

[13] Servant of God Lucia Dos Santos, as quoted in Robert Feeney, *The Rosary: "The Little Summa*," 4th ed. (USA: Aquinas Press, 2003), 112.

Chapter 10

[14] G.K. Chesterton, *The Autobiography of G.K. Chesterton* (San Francisco: Ignatius Press, 2006), 217.

[15] Attributed to St. Augustine in *Manipulus Florum* (c. 1306), a Medieval Latin handbook edited by Thomas Hibernicus.

Chapter 11

[16] Pope John Paul II, *Dives in Misericordia* (*God Who is Rich in Mercy*), Encyclical Letter, November 30, 1980, http://w2.vatican.va/content/john-paulii/en/encyclicals/documents/ hf_jp-ii_enc_30111980_dives-in-misericordia.html.